GETTING STARTED WITH
GIS
A LITA Guide

Eva Dodsworth

Neal-Schuman Publishers, Inc.

New York   London

Don't miss this book's companion website!

To access additional resources and hands-on tutorials, GIS data, links to interactive mapping programs, as well as updates to the tutorials provided in the book, go to:

http://www.neal-schuman.com/gis

Published by Neal-Schuman Publishers, Inc.
100 William St., Suite 2004
New York, NY 10038

Printed and bound in the United States of America.

The paper used in this publication meets the minimum requirements of American National Standard for Information Sciences—Permanence of Paper for Printed Library Materials, ANSI Z39.48-1992.

Library of Congress Cataloging-in-Publication Data

Dodsworth, Eva, 1976-
   Getting started with GIS : a LITA guide / Eva Dodsworth.
      p. cm. — (LITA guide ; #18)
   Includes bibliographical references and index.
   ISBN 978-1-55570-775-0 (alk. paper)
   1. Libraries—Special collections—Geographic information systems. 2. Geographic information systems. I. Title.

Z688.G33D63 2012
025.2'7910285—dc23

                                                        2011039125

Contents

iii

iv

List of Figures

vii

ix

Preface

Library professionals continuously expand their skills and embrace new technologies in order to better connect with and serve users. One of the latest technologies to enter the mainstream information economy is online geographic applications (Web Mapping 2.0). This geographic information web mapping explosion has produced a new generation, GeoWeb users, who are skilled in reading, using, and creating online maps. They enjoy spatial relations and have the desire to find and display the geographic locations of their themes of interest. They expect interactivity and the ability to quickly and easily communicate and share their findings with others.

Both scholars and the general public are becoming widely interested in using mapping technologies for professional and personal purposes. Spatial literacy and geographic awareness are fundamental life skills to have in today's modern day and age. To successfully connect with others, spatial literacy needs to be developed in all members of society, especially those in teaching and information services roles. As a social, organizational, and communication tool, digital mapping, or Geographic Information System (GIS) technology, is becoming integrated into many online applications and resources, and yet very few library professionals are trained to use this technology. GIS is found across many disciplines and is no longer the restricted purview of GIS and map librarians. More and more, library reference staff are being asked location-based questions, as community users and scholars delve comfortably into the modern mapping world. To properly embed spatial resources into the library's pool of information resources, however, some background knowledge is required.

Getting Started with GIS: A LITA Guide was written for library staff working at academic, public, and special libraries, as well as for students studying communication and information science. This book is aimed specifically for all library staff who deliver information and reference services. It is designed to help readers understand, utilize, and embed mapping technology into the services they offer—whether it be a reference service, an outreach program, or a library digitization project. Through theory and simple step-by-step instructions, library professionals will receive an introduction to GIS and mapping experience using several online applications. This book serves as a complete training package for all library staff interested in gaining the most up-to-date and relevant web mapping skills.

Getting Started with GIS was developed using content that I teach at several Library and Information Science (LIS) programs. A handful of LIS programs already offer GIS and mapping courses, preparing the new librarian for modern day user needs. Although new librarians are entering the field trained in the latest and greatest technologies, experienced library staff members often don't have the same opportunity. This is the first book of its kind to teach non-GIS librarians GIS and mapping skills, filling the knowledge gap between those recently graduated and those in the field for a number of years.

The ultimate goal of this book is to train readers on the use of mapping technology in libraries, enhancing their reference skills and expanding their liaison and teaching services. Specifically, the mapping skills that will be acquired include:

- Be able to answer simple mapping and/or GIS-related questions at the reference desk
- Recognize GIS-related classroom opportunities
- Teach mapping skills to others
- Promote mapping and GIS technologies and services
- Enjoy GIS in your own personal life

Organization

Getting Started with GIS: A LITA Guide features six chapters that provide the reader with examples, ideas, and hands-on tutorials to develop spatial information literacy skills, working knowledge of popular mapping programs, and ideas of how to embed GIS into library services and programs. A **companion website (http://www.neal-schuman.com/gis)** also accompanies this book and offers additional resources and hands-on tutorials, providing the reader with further training and a collection of online resources.

Chapter 1 begins with an overview of recommended geo-related skills that all service-oriented library professionals should possess. Readers are introduced to geographic literacy, where they are shown how maps are prevalent in daily tasks and routines. The concept that geographic awareness and spatial literacy has become a "life skill" is introduced. This chapter discusses the importance of librarians being able to speak the same "language" as their library users. To communicate effectively, to market the library successfully, and to implement a fresh and relative information literacy program, library professionals must have some familiarity with modern geo-technology. A suggested list of skills and competencies will assist in the library's development of training programs, as well as for individual professional development. The recommended geo-skill set will provide all library professionals with the skills to independently respond to geo-related requests without being dependent on mapping or GIS professionals.

Chapter 2 provides an overview of the types of geographic and GIS-based applications that are available online. Readers are introduced to a number of different online interactive maps, with hands-on tutorials that lead them to using a variety of different types of online maps—static, interactive, and personalized maps. Readers are provided with easy to follow step-by-step instructions for creating their own personal online maps. Maps used in mobile applications are also discussed, and an easy to understand introduction to GIS technology and software is provided. The reader will gain an understanding of how all of these applications can be applied to academic, professional, and personal purposes.

Chapter 3 provides the reader with a detailed overview of some of the more popular online mapping programs. Users learn the ins and outs of Google Earth, and through hands-on exercises they learn how to create map mashups and how to easily embed maps into library websites. These applications will prove to be powerful map making tools for library professionals wishing to create maps for visualizing information for presentations, events, and webpages and for creating digital projects. Readers will also find these tutorials useful in their reference work, teaching, and training programs.

Chapter 4 introduces the reader to GIS data and GIS software programs and their accessibility in libraries. This chapter provides readers with the geospatial literacy skills needed to comfortably and confidently meet the basic GIS needs of users. Hands-on tutorials using the proprietary software ArcGIS and the free open source software QGIS are included, guiding readers to creating professional looking maps.

Chapter 5 examines how GIS technology can be incorporated into library services for the purposes of exposing and delivering library collections. Using examples from several libraries, readers are introduced to the concept of digitizing their library collections for the purposes of online retrieval. GIS technology has greatly influenced the ways libraries are offering collection search, discovery, and distribution methodology and tools. This chapter also includes tutorials for how to use applications to geotag library material with a locational component, as well as how to convert spatial files into Keyhole Markup Language (KML) formats.

Chapter 6 examines how libraries utilize GIS technology and mapping resources in library programs, in teaching, and in learning. This chapter also offers considerations for establishing basic GIS information service and training opportunities for library staff.

Getting Started with GIS: A LITA Guide also includes a glossary of terms used in the book, as well as a content-rich **companion website (http://www.neal-schuman .com/gis)** offering additional tutorials and access to GIS data and links to interactive mapping programs. Updates to the tutorials provided in this book will be made available on this website.

Getting Started with GIS: A LITA Guide looks at how traditional library services are expanding to include GIS resources and how library programs are being enhanced by the inclusion of GIS technology in the planning and delivery of them. From offering Google Earth workshops to geocaching activities, to seminars on using maps for genealogical research, libraries are introducing their users to mapping and GIS-based resources. Libraries are a source of information and education, as demonstrated by their offering of training seminars, instruction support, and personal assistance in finding and using map-based resources. *Getting Started with GIS: A LITA Guide* provides relevant examples, ideas, and the training necessary to upgrade your library service to include GIS-based mapping technology.

Acknowledgments

This book could not have been written without the curiosity, passion, and dedication of the many library school students I have been fortunate enough to work with. Their questions and desire to learn have prompted the creation of this book. I am also very grateful to my colleagues in the public and academic library systems who have provided me with their mapping stories, experiences, and challenges. Many of their own projects have been shared in this book.

I would also like to express my deepest gratitude to the staff at the University of Waterloo Library for their gracious support and insightful ideas. Specifically, I would like to thank Richard Pinnell and Mark Haslett, as well as my colleagues at the University Map Library who have all worked extra hard during my absence.

I have had the most wonderful experience learning from my editor from Neal-Schuman, Sandy Wood. Thank you so much for your interest, dedication, and accessibility.

This book could not have been written without the immense support from my loving husband, Dave, my girls, Emily and Alyvia, and my canine boys, Russell and Darwin, who have all been extremely patient and independent throughout the duration of researching and writing this book. Dave, your insight and common-sense evaluation of my ideas have always grounded me. Lastly, I'd like to thank my parents, Zygmunt and Margaret Hobot, for their daily support since day one. Even though GIS is sometimes GSI to you, you have always been positive and extremely encouraging about all my ideas. Thank you so much.

* * *

Chapter 1

Background

Web Mapping: For the New Generation of Internet Users

Geographic information technology is becoming a central component for managing, analyzing, and visualizing the world's information (Tuttle, Anderson, and Huff, 2008). Everyday information is being mapped, or geo-located, by mainstream society—traffic flows, location of events, placemarks, photos, videos, trail routes, taxi fare estimations, personal information, and more. With its ease of use and accessibility, online mapping has expanded the realm of communication and information sharing.

Since 2005, when Google, Microsoft, and Yahoo! released free web mapping applications, the rate of growth and interest in web mapping technology has skyrocketed (Rouse, Bergeron, and Harris, 2007). Easy access to spatial information and map overlays has provided users with the means to understand their world, neighborhoods, and communities of interest. Internet users now have access to location-based information for the entire world. From small details about their neighborhood to an interior glimpse of museums across the countries, users have become more culturally and geographically aware. The increase in society's environmental and geographical literacy stems from GeoWeb 2.0 applications such as Google Earth and Google Maps.

> **GeoWeb 2.0**
>
> The GeoWeb is a collection of online applications, manifested on the World Wide Web that uses interactive, dynamic web services based on geographic or location-based technology (Maguire, 2007).

1

Google mapping products offer users free access to images of the world—from satellite images to photographs taken at the street level. Not only have companies like Google enlightened society by popularizing the notion of mapping geographic locations, they have provided users with the tools to teach students geography—particularly about culture, the environment, and map skills (Senise, 2010). However, it certainly doesn't stop at geography—teachers are incorporating Google Earth into subjects such as math (Petra, 2010), geology, literature, physics, art, history, climatology, and more (Kerski, 2009). Refer to the website How to Teach with Google Earth (http://serc.carleton.edu/sp/library/google_earth/how.html) for specific examples, as well as Google for Educators (http://www.google.com/educators/geo_class.html).

Outside of teaching, the majority of Internet users have dabbled with mapping applications for driving directions and more recently for business searches. MapQuest (http:www.mapquest.com/) is used by more than 40 million unique users each month (Crum, 2010). As of 2009, Microsoft Bing Maps (http://www.bing.com/maps/) had 83.3 million users monthly (Singel, 2009), and in 2010 Google Maps had hit 100 million monthly users on their mobile applications alone (Boulton, 2010).

Both young and old are using GeoWeb applications. In 2009, the Nielson Company conducted a survey of U.S. seniors' use of the Internet. They found that 68.6 percent of seniors spent their time on the web, viewing or printing online maps. This was the number two online activity, with number one being checking personal e-mail (*Nielson Wire*, 2009).

Society's interest in maps goes beyond viewing maps and querying for directions, however. Some have developed quite the interest in conducting their own surveys, forming niche groups, and mapping their findings for all to see. Citizen mapping, or volunteered geographic information (VGI), has become very popular among individuals and groups who enthusiastically work together to create highly specialized and detailed maps (Swift, 2010). Working with the premise that locals know their locality better than anybody else, it may not be long before every square inch of the world will be mapped and annotated—from the pool in your backyard to the maple tree in the front.

> **Volunteered Geographic Information**
>
> Volunteered geographic information, citizen mapping, volunteer cartography, and map crowdsourcing are popular terms used to describe amateur mapmakers who contribute their knowledge of place and space in GeoWeb applications to build highly detailed maps. OpenStreetMap (http://www.openstreetmap.org/) is an example of an online world map that has contributors adding mapping objects such as infrastructure, natural features, and points of interest (parks, churches, schools, etc.).

Today, there are millions of location-based applications available on the web. Whether used for business or pleasure, several applications can map specific topics of interest. Some offer users the ability to add their own data with customizable end results, while others offer a wealth of resources from a data bank. Textual information is being replaced or supplemented by interactive maps, as is demonstrated by many company and organization webpages. For example, all levels of government across various sectors now embed interactive mapping technology into their websites. Many municipal and county websites describe locations of their services with interactive maps that allow users to search for properties, walking trails, parks, libraries, public transit, pools, and other municipal information. Examples of several municipal webpages using interactive mapping technology can be found from the State of Connecticut's Geospatial Information Systems Council's webpage (http://www.ct.gov/gis/cwp/view.asp?a=2681&q=328088). State and provincial governments offer web-based mapping applications that distribute information related to themes

2

of the environment, water, geology, soils, agriculture, infrastructure, emergency responses, and so forth.

Social media as well use mapping technology to entice users to get involved and participate in their surveys and activities. For example, Foursquare and Google launched a map visualization application that tracked the number of voters at all of

> **About Foursquare**
>
> Foursquare is a location-based web and mobile application that enables users to geotag their locations on their mobile devices and post to Twitter and/or Facebook. Some events and activities award points and badges to participants upon "checking in" (*Wikipedia*, 2010a).

the polling stations in the 2010 U.S. election. Additionally, Foursquare badges were awarded to voters at the polls, encouraging them to "check in" their poll location and post their voting status to their friends on Twitter and/or Facebook. This type of location-based social media activity is hoped to increase voter participation (Carr, 2010).

Blogs and social network sites are also incorporating mapping technology into their pages. Facebook, for example uses maps in several applications—Bing Maps is used in the Place Location Service application, and Google Maps Latitude is used in the Footprint Feed application. Both applications map the locational information supplied by the user. There's also a geosocial network application that combines both social networking and mapping. ZoomAtlas (http://www.zoomatlas.com/) provides a map that can be updated by the user—from roads and sidewalks to miniscule details like grass and house bricks. The social networking aspect of it, however, allows users to leave notes at specific locations on the maps. The users post these notes to others who may share similar experiences or have answers to questions about a location on the map, such as history of home owners or school alumnus.

This web mapping explosion has produced a new generation of Internet, or GeoWeb, users. They are skilled in reading, using, and creating online maps. They enjoy spatial relations and have the desire to find and display the geographic locations of their themes of interest. They expect interactivity and the ability to quickly and easily communicate and share their findings with others.

Library professionals have the opportunity to take advantage of this evolving technology and the interests that library users have in it. Transforming the library professional into a geoliterate service provider will open the communication channel to a whole new level. The ability for library staff to attract and communicate with their library users is an essential ingredient to a successful library program. This chapter examines the number of ways that libraries can incorporate mapping technology into their programs, collections, and promotional campaigns. The reader will gain an understanding of the value of inheriting geospatial literacy skills for the purposes of connecting with their users as well as for enhancing library services. The remaining chapters in this book will focus on training and developing library staff into modern geoliterate professionals.

3

Geographic Information System (GIS) Technology

Until now, geographic applications have mainly been described here as "mapping applications" or "GeoWeb" tools. All of the applications discussed so far are using Geographic Information System (GIS) technology. Often, when one thinks of a GIS, a complex software program comes to mind. GIS is often used by professionals for purposes of managing, manipulating, and analyzing geospatial data. It is of course also used by many for map making. What many Internet users don't realize is that they themselves are using

> **Geographic Information System (GIS)**
>
> Geographic Information System (GIS) is a set of tools that captures, stores, analyzes, manages, and presents data that are linked to location (*Wikipedia*, 2010b).

> **Spatial or Data Analysis**
>
> Spatial or data analysis is a geographical study of the spatial visualization of patterns, properties, and relationships. Examples of variables that are often analyzed include population demographics, quality of life indexes, illness distributions, and business sales (Câmara et al., 2001).

GIS technology, but in a more user friendly online format. This book introduces GIS to the readers through the more recent releases of WebGIS—online mapping programs that are fueled by GIS technology. Chapter 4 is dedicated to desktop GIS, where readers will gain an introduction to cartography and data management and analysis.

Stemming originally from a sophisticated desktop program, the common misconception is that GIS is a difficult and complicated application used by cartographers and geographers. Although historically it was used primarily by these specific users, GIS has proven beneficial to a wide variety of disciplines, professions, and user groups. GIS is used extensively in government, business, and research in a wide variety of applications, such as demographic analysis, infrastructure planning, business marketing and site location development, real estate analysis, demographic analysis, and much more (*Wikipedia*, 2010b).

The transition from desktop software to online applications has certainly exposed the concept of geospatial visualization, with many user groups dabbling with their own web mapping servers and interactive mapping programs and creating their own open source software programs. In fact, many open source GIS programs are stripped down of their analysis capabilities, making them simply only mapping programs. With the majority of society's interest being in mapping, and not spatial analysis, GIS applications are now being built to attract the map making audience. Easy to access and simple to learn applications are available for both new and expert users. These types of applications allow information to be mapped, giving the potential for problem solving and decision making. They also offer everybody the ability to create a map easily and quickly without the need for professional cartographic skills and in a highly visual and interactive way.

There are now millions of websites across North America that use GIS technology in online webpages and applications. The interactivity of these applications has certainly developed over the past couple of years as well, offering users the ability to create and share sophisticated, dynamic, customized maps. Society has popularized the notion of mapping everything "because you can." If an entity can be defined in geographical terms, then it can be mapped. Every one of us can be placed on a map, and everything and everybody related to us can be as well—our home, our library, our favourite coffee shop, our family photos, the settings of the novels we read, the stores we buy our groceries in, and so forth.

A GIS program imports information from a table (a database file) and displays it in a visual format. For example, it can take a list of public and academic library locations and display it as a collection of points on a map. It can also take a list of bus stops and bus routes and map those locations as well. Now, one can analyze the relationship of the two files to determine whether a bookmobile or interlibrary service needs to be established for those libraries with less convenient public transit access. All that is needed in the table is a geographic location, such as a street address, street intersection, or geographic coordinates.

Today, many people are using Global Positioning System (GPS) technology to record locations. Several mobile devices now have GPS receivers built in, and several GPS applications are also available to make location tracking easier. Mobile devices such as the Blackberry and iPhone have GPS chips that enable users to track their locations. Several mobile applications have been created utilizing the GIS and GPS technology. With the ability to track places visited, record distances walked, and tag interesting finds, it's no wonder that people are captivated by this ability to effortlessly record, visualize, and share their world travels.

5

Many mapping applications available allow users to access live traffic information, map their current location, and of course receive turn-by-turn directions. Other mapping applications include live weather maps and business and demographic information from Business Analyst Online (BAO), and several geographic games and quizzes like GeoMaster (Eisenman, 2009) and Geography Brainscape (CNET, 2010) help build geographic literacy. GIS software companies have also recently released mobile versions of their GIS programs, along with toolkits that allow others to build their own mapping applications.

Society's vast interest in mapping and GIS technology has expanded into the mobile industry, where users can continually use and create and update maps throughout their day. Because of the ease, people are using maps more than they were when only paper versions were available. Being able to trace their daily moves and inquire about the space around them helps develop the spatial language skills that many others are using and communicating with.

Spatial literacy and geographic awareness are fundamental life skills to have in today's modern day and age. To successfully connect with others, spatial literacy needs to be developed in all members of society, especially those in teaching and information services roles.

Using GeoWeb 2.0 to Connect with Library Users

Tagging geographic locations to information is a convenient and effective way to communicate a great deal of information in a relatively quick amount of time. Organizations, including libraries, are increasingly taking advantage of this technology to connect with their users. As often is the case with libraries and other information resources, the key to user satisfaction is to be a step ahead of the technological curve and offer services that include or use modern, popular, and cutting edge technology. For example, many libraries have gone beyond paper books and in-person reference services and are now offering iPod rentals and e-book readers and transferring information through social media like Instant Messenger, Facebook, and Twitter (Harris, 2010). In additional to these Web 2.0 tools, some libraries are also implementing GeoWeb 2.0 technology into their library promotion and delivery of services. Interested in the latest and greatest tools available, librarians are often looking for new and exciting ways to connect with their users (Brown, 2008). Librarians search for new media to promote resources and services, to incorporate into course assignments, and to use during teaching and training.

Quite a bit of research has been conducted over the past few years on the uses and benefits of Web 2.0 applications in libraries. Libraries tend to use a handful of the same social tools, which closely parallel the ones used most by library users. Curtis Rogers (2009) conducted a survey of American library staff members to determine the variety of Web 2.0 and social networking sites utilized to promote library services and programs. Among the highest ranked were Facebook (71.4 percent), Flickr (49.6 percent), and blogs (47.4 percent), followed by Twitter and Meebo (36.1 percent) and YouTube (35.3 percent). The survey did not include mapping based Web 2.0 applications, which was found to be a common omission among surveys studied.

A search on the web revealed the number of users registered with the mentioned Web 2.0 applications. As of 2010, Facebook had 500 million active users (Facebook, 2010); Flickr had 24 million users registered (Statsaholic, 2010); Twitter had 105 million users (Ostrow, 2010); and YouTube had 258 million registered users (Lake, 2011). Astonishingly, Google Earth has had over 600 million downloads (Taylor, 2010), surpassing even the number of Facebook users. These statistics reflect the importance of expanding the typical Web 2.0 collection of applications to include some of the more popular mapping ones. Keeping the importance of the library-to-user connection in mind, it's worthwhile investigating how libraries can incorporate popular mapping applications into the library's communication, research, and teaching campaigns.

6

Joe Murphy and Heather Moulaison (2009) suggested a set of competencies that librarians should possess as social networking–literate information professionals. Some of the skills identified included successfully navigating relevant online social networking sites; capability of creating, contributing, and revising content in various formats; and, very importantly, capability of teaching these skills to library patrons and colleagues. Since none of Murphy and Moulaison's examples included any mention of mapping, or location-based applications, it's essential to build on their reflections and use their outlined competencies as a framework for establishing similar proficiencies that relate to the GeoWeb 2.0 applications.

Recommended Skill Set for Geoliterate Library Professionals

Interest in geographic information and related technology used to be limited to cartographers and geographers. Today, mapping or geographic technology has the attention of people with a wide range of backgrounds and demographics. Anybody off the street can walk into a library and ask a map or location-related question. There are some academic libraries that have map or GIS librarians who can assist with higher level mapping queries and technologies. The types of questions that may be asked by library users don't always exclusively require a map or GIS librarian's assistance. Training library staff in basic GIS skills or geographic literacy will provide them with the skills necessary to meet the mapping needs of users, colleagues, and administrators.

The recommended skills for geoliterate library professionals apply to staff offering services in any type of library. They have been created to assist in the development of training programs, as well as for individual professional development. The goals and proficiencies have been compiled of the essential skills that library professionals would find beneficial to have in delivering knowledgeable and confident geo-related library services. The following recommended geo-skill set will provide all library professionals with the skills to independently respond to geo-related requests without being dependent on mapping or GIS professionals.

The broader skills of a geoliterate library professional include these:

- Understanding the importance of communication with maps and being able to communicate effectively with other map users
- Utilizing popular GeoWeb tools to promote and outreach to library users
- Having a working knowledge of popular GeoWeb tools to respond to library clients' reference questions
- Utilizing popular GeoWeb tools in the classroom and within the course curriculum for use in research, presentation, and evaluation
- Being able to teach GeoWeb mapping skills to others
- Being able to evaluate and recommend GeoWeb applications

The three recommended skills set for geoliterate library professionals consists of the following:

1. **Maintain geographic awareness and spatial literacy:** develop basic spatial literacy skills; understand the importance and effectiveness of communicating with maps and location-based technology; stay current with the widely used GeoWeb applications; and have knowledge of the programs' major features
2. **Utilize web mapping applications:** have working knowledge of popular mapping applications, including ability to use major features; and incorporate the products into library services
3. **Incorporate GeoWeb 2.0 into library's information literacy initiatives:** teach geographic information literacy; teach use of GeoWeb mapping applications; teach with GeoWeb mapping technology

Many library professionals begin their careers without any formal training in geographic applications. Mapping is covered in depth in GIS-related courses that are offered in only a handful of ALA-accredited library programs (Dodsworth, 2009). In 2009, Dodsworth conducted a curriculum review of all the ALA-accredited Master of Library and Information Science (MLIS) programs to identify courses that trained students on the applications of GIS technology in libraries. Of the 57 programs, only four offered courses specific to GIS in libraries. All four courses had similar objectives, including training librarians to answer basic map-related reference questions. This involved GIS application training—both online and desktop.

With clearly so few library school programs offering exposure to GIS technology, it is imperative that some other form of training is made available to library professionals. The recommended three-tiered skill set may be used as a framework for establishing a training program for library professionals.

Maintain Geographic Awareness and Spatial Literacy

An essential life skill is the ability to use the properties of space to communicate, reason, and solve problems. Most people have already developed geographic and spatial literacy skills through geographic education. They are able to use location for organizing and discovering information. They have been taught to comprehend and analyze maps and to be able to read them like text in a book. They have been taught to understand graphical design (e.g., symbols on a map) and to deduce conclusions and make decisions based on information displayed in the map. Spatial literacy is a highly valued fundamental prerequisite skill for successful communication and utilization of spatial technologies. As the National Research Council (NRC) stated in *Learning to Think Spatially*, "without explicit attention to [spatial literacy], we cannot meet our responsibility for equipping the next generation of students for life and work in the 21st century" (NRC, 2006: 1).

Geographic awareness is the fundamental understanding that every place has a space and that potentially everything on the earth can be recorded as a geographic location and hence can be displayed in a visual format. Geographic awareness includes being cognizant of society's wants and needs for mapping tools and applications and staying current with the latest social trends as they relate to these needs. It is clear based on the number of maps we see daily that society finds great value in graphical searching, indexing, and presentation methods. Unlike text, maps provide many users with a graphic that cuts across cultural, social, and geographical differences.

Utilize Web Mapping Applications

Library professionals should be fairly knowledgeable about the types of mapping applications that are available and their main features. They should be able to utilize the tools to assist patrons, if needed, as well as use the tools in their own project work. The next sections describe some of the ways libraries and library professionals use web mapping applications.

Mapping for Library Use

Library professionals are in a position to employ the benefits of map communication in a number of ways. First, they can use GeoWeb technologies to aid the work they do in their positions. For example, they may be inclined to create a customized map of the campus for visitors or conference delegates. Or they may need to promote a special event and map its location on a library's webpage or blog or on Facebook.

Some library professionals are also beginning to use virtual globes like Google Earth for library promotion and service delivery. There are currently many completed projects that library staff have created that incorporate Google Earth for the purposes of organizing, storing, and displaying library resources. Several libraries, such as Carleton University Library (CUL, 2010), Yale University Library (YUL, 2010), and the Perry-Castañeda Library at the University of Texas at Austin (UTA, 2010) have digitized their collection indexes (air photos, fire insurance plans, and topographic maps, respectively) and presented them to their library users in the Google Earth–read Keyhole Markup Language (KML) format. The University of Waterloo Library (Dodsworth, 2008), and Arizona State University Library (ASUL, 2010) have digitized their historical air photos and made them available for viewing with Google Earth. These files are accessible from their library websites, and once downloaded the photos can be viewed in the virtual globe.

Maps have been digitized and made available for Google Earth viewing as well. For example, the Library of Congress offers its Hotchkiss Map Collection in KML format (LC, 2010), and the British Library shares its Google Earth–supported British historical map collection (BL, 2010). With a significantly increasing rate, more and more libraries are using Google Earth

9

technology to highlight their collections. Terry Ballard (2009), for example, discussed one library that created KML placemarks to lead users to its library collection of urban planning documents. This type of collection entry increases exposure to digital collections.

> **Keyhole Markup Language (KML)**
>
> KML is a geographic file format that displays data primarily in Google Earth and Google Maps, although it is increasingly becoming supported by other mapping applications as well. KML files can be viewed in, created in, and exported from Google Earth. A KML file can consist of raster data such as an image or photograph or vector data such as a point, line, or polygon. It can also consist of text and hyperlinks.

A number of libraries also use Google Maps to embed customized maps into their websites. The Kitchener Public Library in Ontario, for example, uses Google maps to show the geographic coverage of its historical photograph collection (KPL, 2010). The McMillan Memorial Library in Wisconsin has several Google Map projects showcasing its historical photographs and postcards, as well as local cemetery locations (Barnett, 2009, 2010a,b).

With its customizable features, libraries opt to use Google Maps to display locations of points of interest. The Franklin Park Public Library in Illinois created an online map using the My Maps feature of Google Maps. It mapped the locations of the local landmarks that reference desk staff are most often asked about by library patrons. In lieu of explaining the directions to the landmarks, staff now use the map to answer these types of directional questions (Jacobson, 2008). Other popular maps created by public libraries include locations of historical landmarks, genealogical family trees of locals, and of course maps of library locations.

Mapping technology has also been used quite a bit for library administrative purposes. Mapping and GIS technology have been used to find future library users, to help make collection purchasing decisions, to analyze library services, and to manage space. The Colorado State Library and the public libraries in Colorado, for example, have created mapping projects that displayed the geographic distribution of their library users. They combined the geographic locations of their users with community demographics to assist in management decision making (Wrede, 2006). There are many more examples of web mapping as it relates to library promotion and delivery of services, and this will be discussed in detail throughout the next several chapters.

Mapping in Reference Services

For the library to remain a respected information resource, it's critical that the service mirrors the information needs of the users. Both scholars and the general public are becoming widely interested in taking advantage of mapping technologies for professional and personal purposes.

One of the more common uses of mapping technology includes geotagging, the process of assigning geographic locations to records like photos and images.

The video and image hosting site Flickr announced in 2009 that its users have geotagged over 100 million photos (Flickr, 2009). Many disciplines take advantage of geotagged georeferenced records—whether they

> **Georeferencing**
>
> Georeferencing is a procedure used to establish the spatial location of an object (image, map, document, etc.) by linking its position to the earth's surface.

be text documents, personal photos, or historical maps and air photos, users are geotagging and georeferencing them to relative locations on the earth. Library users may inquire about application options and instructions on how to geotag their vacation photos, cemetery inscriptions, or other projects.

Another common use of maps is the exploration and navigation of virtual globes such as Google Earth. Library users may ask reference questions about accessing KML files, sharing content, and understanding Google imagery copyright. Some library users may wish to create customized maps and embed them in their webpages or school projects. Popular among library users is finding locations of points of interest such as walking trails, leash-free parks, locations of businesses, directions to skating rinks, and so forth. A trained reference staff member would be able to point to map resources online to answer some of these types of questions. All of these examples and more will be covered in greater detail in the upcoming chapters.

Mapping for Classroom Use

Library professionals may wish to utilize their mapping skills by incorporating mapping technology into course curriculums or classrooms. Library professionals can share their knowledge with faculty members, instructors, and teachers and together create guides and assignments that utilize the mapping applications as resources for research, communication, and presentation.

At university and college libraries, many faculty across several disciplines consult their subject librarians to discuss resources for courses (Frank et al., 2001). A greater number of faculty are also incorporating mapping technologies into their course curriculum, and the subject librarian may be expected to know about the geo-resources that pertain to their subject specialty. There are many mapping resources of interest to historians, archaeologists, genealogists, biologists, environmentalists, planners, engineers, architects, artists, and so forth. This too will be discussed further in the upcoming chapters.

Public library professionals also have the opportunity to work with students and teachers. The sheer number of K–12 mapping exercises available in blogs and websites created for and by teachers demonstrates the popularity of it in classroom settings. Google Earth is often used to teach spatial literacy, as well as geographic awareness. Students explore the virtual world to learn about native species of plant life, effects of natural disasters, water resources, and human culture.

Aside from Google, millions of other static and interactive maps online can be used in the classroom. The National Geographic Society (http://maps .nationalgeographic.com/maps) offers a large collection of thematic maps for the entire world (trails, atlases, weather, historical, etc.). The U.S. Census Bureau (http://quickfacts.census.gov/qfd/index.html), Statistics Canada (http://geodepot .statcan.ca/GeoSearch2006/GeoSearch2006.jsp?resolution=H&lang=E& otherLang=F), and the CIA World Factbook (https://www.cia.gov/library/ publications/the-world-factbook/geos/co.html) offer demographic maps. The David Rumsey Collection offers one of the largest private collections of historical maps, many of which have been georeferenced and made available in Google Earth (http://www.davidrumsey.com/about/david-rumsey).

Many students and teachers across all levels of education also adopt desktop GIS programs in the course curriculum. Instead of searching for online tools that meet their classroom criteria, they use their own datasets with a GIS program that maps, manages, and analyzes their themes.

One final example of how public libraries can incorporate mapping technology into their services is through location-based games. Geocaching, for example, is an activity that both teachers and librarians like to run, offering students a fun, interactive way to promote library resources, learn about the local community, and work together as a team. Geocaching is an excellent way to introduce people to the concept of virtual worlds and geographic awareness.

The Public Library of Charlotte & Mecklenburg County, in Charlotte, North Carolina, used the geocaching game to introduce new library users to five of the city's library locations by hiding treasures across town.

> **Geocaching**
>
> Geocaching is a recreational outdoor activity that has participants looking for hidden containers using a navigational tool such as a GPS device.

Library staff were trained to use the GPS devices, which were rented from the Geospatial Information & Technology Association (Czarnecki, 2009).

Incorporate GeoWeb Technology into Library Information Literacy Initiatives

Geoliteracy goes beyond the fundamental understanding that geography and society are interwoven and gets into more specific uses of geography by society. Geoliteracy includes being cognizant of the more popular online mapping tools and applications available and knowing how they are and can be used by library patrons and colleagues. Again, understanding the potential of these programs will benefit the library user and the library. Knowing that one can integrate a map onto a Facebook page, for example, may encourage the library professional to create a map of library locations to promote an event. Knowing that a specific online resource can help locate all of the grocery stores in the city may assist the professor who is teaching a course in retail. Some experience with the features within the application may assist the library professional when asked certain reference questions—for example, explaining how to add coordinate information to a list of addresses, draw the boundary of a study area, or add a map widget to a blog.

Regardless of subject specialty, library professionals work collaboratively to foster independent and lifelong learners. Information literacy skills are taught in a number of different ways and formats, and since the public release of online mapping tools, many libraries have been including this technology as a gateway to information. Recently there has been a shift from teaching specific courses about specific resources to broadening the research pool to allow students to use their critical thinking skills to decide for themselves which resources would suit them best. Currently, many library professionals are not including GeoWeb applications into their library's information literacy initiatives. It is therefore imperative to consider this important concept and begin integrating it into information literacy planning and delivery efforts.

Introducing Library Users to GeoWeb and Mapping Technology

GeoWeb technology can be introduced to students in a number of ways—through information literacy courses, workshops, online tutorials, events, or course-integrated instruction. One can also teach *with* the technology. A traditional library presentation can be made more visually appealing to the audience if the slides are embedded into an application with high visuals and support for animations. There are mapping applications that offer dynamic presentation tools that can be used when discussing anything related to locations, society, and the environment. Maps can be used to showcase areas of interest, and mapping applications can be used to demonstrate the ease of communicating, sharing, and storing visual information.

Acquiring Geoliteracy Skills

As mentioned earlier, GIS and mapping literacy skills are not often taught in MLIS programs. In fact, because web mapping technology is still fairly new, no documented libraries have implemented their own training programs yet. Upgrading library skills is possible through workshops, seminars, and online tutorials, and it may be best for library professionals to use the tutorials and exercises in this book as part of their library training program. The tutorials included in this book were created to specifically help library professionals across different libraries to develop basic GIS and mapping skills.

Information literacy programs will continue to evolve and change with the times and with the needs of library users. The most challenging part is being able to anticipate what the users' needs are and then satisfy those needs through ways that are refreshing, cutting edge, and relevant to their studies and interests. Educated and knowledgeable library users are rarely formed without the influence of the library's staff and resources. This is why it is imperative that an ongoing training program is established to refresh and upgrade skills on a regular basis.

13

Conclusion

Information literacy development is an ongoing progression toward the fulfillment of skills required in today's technology-heavy society. As discussed in this chapter, spatial literacy and map communication are essential skills that are being developed in many members of society. The use of mapping applications does not end at the high school, college, or university level, but simply begins to flourish then. The use of and dependence on maps as information and communication tools certainly continues into many adult lives and professional careers.

For libraries to support the needs of today's modern users, library staff themselves need to gain the spatial and mapping skills necessary to fulfill user request, and to be able to implement the technology into library projects and services. This chapter has discussed the relevant geoliteracy skills that library professionals need to develop. The next chapter will introduce the reader to geographic and GIS awareness, the foundation of spatial communication. Users will get a sense of how online mapping applications are being used daily for personal use and in education and libraries.

References

ASUL (Arizona State University Libraries). 2010. "Aerial Photography." Arizona State University Libraries. Accessed November 11. http://lib.asu.edu/mapcoll/airphoto.

Ballard, Terry. 2009. "Inheriting the Earth: Using KML Files to Add Placemarks Relating to the Library's Original Content to Google Earth and Google Maps." *New Library World* 110, no. 7/8: 357–365.

Barnett, Andy. 2009. "Bonnie Young Postcard Collection." McMillan Memorial Library. Last modified January 31. http://www.mcmillanlibrary.org/history/postcards.html.

———. 2010a. "100 Years of Pictorial & Descriptive History of Wisconsin Rapids, Wisconsin by T.A. Taylor 1934." McMillan Memorial Library. Accessed November 3. http://www.mcmillanlibrary.org/taylor/map.html.

———. 2010b. "Wood County Cemetery Locations and Maps." McMillan Memorial Library. Accessed November 3. http://www.mcmillanlibrary.org/history/cemeteries.html.

BL (British Library). 2010. "Online Gallery—London: A Life in Maps." The British Library Board. Accessed November 11. http://www.bl.uk/londoninmaps.

Boulton, Clint. 2010. "Google Maps for Mobile Surpasses 100M Monthly Users." *eWeek.* http://www.eweek.com/c/a/Mobile-and-Wireless/Google-Maps-for-Mobile-Surpasses-100M-Monthly-Users-142069/.

Brown, Lindy. 2008. "Twittering Libraries." *LIS 5313 Course Wiki* (blog). Fall 2008. http://lis5313.ci.fsu.edu/wiki/index.php/Twittering_Libraries.

Câmara, Gilberto, Antônio Monteiro, Suzana Fucks, and Marília Sá Carvalho. 2001. "Spatial Analysis and GIS: A Primer." A Divisão de Processamento de Imagens (DPI). http://www.dpi.inpe.br/gilberto/tutorials/spatial_analysis/spatial_analysis_primer.pdf.

Carr, Austin. 2010. "Foursquare, Google Launch 'I Voted' Badge." *Fastcompany.* http://www.fastcompany.com/1698253/foursquare-google-mtv-launch-i-voted-badge.

CNET. 2010. "World Geography Crash Course, by Brainscape 1.20100827 for iPhone." CNET. Accessed November 12. http://download.cnet.com/World-Geography-Crash-Course-by-Brainscape/3000-20415_4-75273819.html.

Crum, Chris. 2010. "Driving Traffic with MapQuest and Its New Search Engine: MapQuest Making Improvements to Business Search." *WebProNews*. http://www.webpronews.com/topnews/2010/02/12/driving-traffic-with-mapquest-and-its-new-search-engine.

CUL (Carleton University Library). 2010. "GIS: Interactive Web Indexes for GIS Data." Carleton University Library. Accessed June 28. http://www.library.carleton.ca/gis/web_indexes.htm.

Czarnecki, Kelly. 2009. "The Librarian's Guide to Gaming: An Online Toolkit for Building Gaming @ Your Library." American Library Association. Accessed November 2. http://librarygamingtoolkit.org/plcmcgeocaching.html.

Dodsworth, Eva. 2008. "University of Waterloo Library Air Photo Digitization Project." University of Waterloo. http://www.lib.uwaterloo.ca/locations/umd/project/.

———. 2009. "Developing Geographical and Geospatial Skills in Librarians." *Association of Canadian Map Libraries and Archives Bulletin* 135: 9–13.

Eisenman, Bonnie. 2009. "GeoMaster." *148Apps*. http://www.148apps.com/reviews/geomaster/.

Facebook. 2010. "Press Room: People on Facebook." Facebook. Accessed November 12. http://www.facebook.com/press/info.php?statistics.

Flickr. 2009. "100,000,000 Geotagged Photos (Plus). *Code: Flickr Development Blog*. February 4. http://code.flickr.com/blog/2009/02/04/100000000-geotagged-photos-plus/.

Frank, Donald, Gregory Raschke, Julie Wood, and Julie Yang. 2001. "Information Consulting: The Key to Success in Academic Libraries." *The Journal of Academic Librarianship* 27, no. 2: 90–96.

Harris, Siân. 2010. "Libraries of the Future." *Research Information*. February/March 2010. http://www.researchinformation.info/features/feature.php?feature_id=250.

Jacobson, Mikael. 2008. "Google Maps: You Are Here—Using Google Maps to Bring out Your Library's Local Collections." *Library Journal*. http://www.libraryjournal.com/article/CA6602836.html.

Kerski, Joseph. 2009. "The Implementation and Effectiveness of Geographic Information Systems in Secondary Education." *Journal of Geography* 102: 128–137.

Kincaid, Jason. 2010. "Live: Twitter CEO Ev Williams' Chirp Keynote." *Techcrunch*. http://techcrunch.com/2010/04/14/live-twitter-ceo-ev-williamss-chirp-keynote/.

KPL (Kitchener Public Library). 2010. "KPL Photograph Collection." Kitchener Public Library. Accessed November 9. http://images.ourontario.ca/kitchener/results?grd=444.

Lake, Laura. 2011. "YouTube: Social Media Marketing via Video." About.com. Accessed September 6, 2011. http://marketing.about.com/od/internetmarketing/a/youtubemrktg.htm.

LC (Library of Congress). 2010. "Geography and Map Reading Room: Guides to the Collections." Library of Congress. Accessed March 23. http://www.loc.gov/rr/geogmap/guides.html.

Maguire, David. 2007. "GeoWeb 2.0 and Volunteered GI." Paper presented at the National Center for Geographic Information and Analysis Specialist Meeting on VGI, Santa Barbara, December 13–14.

15

Murphy, Joe, and Heather Moulaison. 2009. "Social Networking Literacy Competencies for Librarians: Exploring Considerations and Engaging Participation." Paper presented at the ACRL 14th National Conference, Seattle, WA, March 12–15.

Nielson Wire. 2009. "Six Million More Seniors Using the Web than Five Years Ago." Nielson Company. http://blog.nielsen.com/nielsenwire/online_mobile/six-million-more-seniors-using-the-web-than-five-years-ago/.

NRC (National Research Council). 2006. *Learning to Think Spatially: GIS as a Support System in the K–12 Curriculum.* 1. Washington, DC: National Academies Press.

Ostrow, Adam. 2010. "Twitter Has 105 Registered Million Users." Mashable. http://mashable.com/2010/04/14/twitter-registered-users/.

Petra, Thomas. 2010. "Real World Math: Using Google Earth in the Math Curriculum." Real World Math. Accessed November 2. http://realworldmath.org/Real_World_Math/RealWorldMath.org.html.

Rogers, Curtis. 2009. "Social Media, Libraries, and Web 2.0: How American Libraries Are Using New Tools for Public Relations and to Attract New Users." Paper presented at the German Library Association Annual Conference Deutscher Bibliothekartag, 2009, in Erfurt, Germany, June 2–5.

Rouse, L., Susan Bergeron, and Trevor Harris. 2007. "Participating in the Geospatial Web: Collaborative Mapping, Social Networks and Participatory GIS." In *The Geospatial Web: How Geobrowsers, Social Software and the Web 2.0 Are Shaping the Network Society*, edited by Arno Scharl and Klaus Tochtermann, 53–158. New York: Springer.

Senise, Mike. 2010. *TeacherTECH: Using Google Earth.* Produced by University of California Television. #18510. http://www.uctv.tv/search-details.aspx?showID=18510&subject=pet.

Singel, Ryan. 2009. "Microsoft Releases New Map App and Bing Features." *Wired.* http://www.wired.com/epicenter/2009/12/bing-new-search/.

Statsaholic. 2010. "Website Traffic Graphs for Flickr." Statsaholic. Accessed April 21. http://www.statsaholic.com/flickr.com.

Swift, Mike. 2010. "Citizen Mapping Gaining Ground." *Seattle Times.* http://seattletimes.nwsource.com/html/businesstechnology/2011756631_maps03.html.

Taylor, Frank. 2010. "Where 2.0—Day 2: Part 1." *Google Earth Blog: The Amazing Things about Google Earth.* http://www.gearthblog.com/index2.html.

Tuttle, Benjamin, Sharolyn Anderson, and Russell Huff. 2008. "Virtual Globes: An Overview of Their History, Uses, and Future Challenges." *Geography Compass* 2, no. 5: 1478–1505.

UTA (University of Texas at Austin). 2010. "Perry-Castañeda Library Map Collection: Army Map Service Topographic Map Series." Last modified March 11. http://www.lib.utexas.edu/maps/ams/.

Wikipedia. 2010a. "Foursquare (Social Networking)." *Wikipedia.* Last modified November 27. http://en.wikipedia.org/wiki/Foursquare_(social_networking).

———. 2010b. "Geographic Information System." *Wikipedia.* Last modified December 3. http://en.wikipedia.org/wiki/Geographic_information_system.

Wrede, Steve. 2006. "Analyzing Library Use Patterns Geospatially: Colorado State Library Conducts a Variety of Projects with GIS." *ArcNews* (Summer). http://www.esri.com/news/arcnews/summer06articles/colorado-state.html.

YUL (Yale University Library). 2010. "New Haven Sanborn Index Maps for Google Earth." Yale University Library. Last modified July 1. http://www.library.yale.edu/MapColl/print_sanborn.html.

Chapter 2

Geographic and GIS Awareness in a Web 2.0 Environment

Introduction: GIS and Internet Applications

Geographic and GIS awareness is the first step toward spatial literacy attainment, as it provides the library professional the background and knowledge of tools necessary to connect with library users. This chapter provides an overview of the types of geographic and GIS-based applications that are available online. The reader will also gain an understanding of how these applications can be applied for academic, professional, and personal purposes.

Incorporating GIS into Our Daily Lives

Most Internet users have had exposure to geographic or GIS-based online applications. One of the most popular uses of these applications is for locating addresses and determining directions. Because of its convenience and ease of use, an increasing number of people are preferring to use the Internet for address searches over the traditional Yellow and White Pages (Felberbaum, 2010). Any point of interest or address search using the Google search engine will result in a map displaying the location of interest. Maps are being embedded in many webpages and over the past few years are including information beyond simple address locations. Internet users have discovered many other practical, valuable, and enjoyable GIS-based webmaps and applications.

If you think about some of the common daily interests that citizens share, you will likely see that those interests have been mapped. Weather conditions, traffic flows, flight routes and schedules, locations of breaking news, locations of latest disease outbreaks, crime, and sexual predators, locations of new and used cars for sale, and so on. Many of these themes have been mapped by individuals using common mapping technologies like Google Maps. So not only do Internet users have easy access to maps of a wide range of topics, but they also have the tools available to create their own maps. Map creation will be discussed in detail in Chapter 3.

Knowing that these types of maps exist and understanding their value is a step toward gaining geographic and GIS awareness. Library professionals are not expected to know all of the mapping resources available, but simply knowing that they do indeed exist may encourage them to search the web for specific applications of interest. For example, if a library user is interested in finding a way to track distance travelled, the trained library professional would have the geographic awareness to know that there is technology available online that can do such a thing. A quick search on the web will find several applications that offer users the ability to draw or enter distances and locations travelled. Figure 2.1 displays the list of results upon inputting the search phrase "map my distance" in Google.

There are mapping applications available for all types of uses. Most users will find applications in their subject matter of interest, whether personal or professional. The following section describes the different types of map resources and mapping applications that are available across a wide range of themes and topics.

Online Map Resources and Applications

Map and GIS resources are used by a number of disciplines and for a wide range of purposes. Students, faculty, and staff at academic institutions are increasingly applying GIS technology in their studies, teachings, and administrative tasks. With mapping and GIS resources available in most academic institutions, many will pay a visit to the library for resources or for assistance in incorporating the technology into project work. Academic library reference staff may see users from history, English, health sciences, and geography, perhaps looking for digital historical, topographic, or thematic maps. Scholars in other disciplines such as psychology, sociology, and business may, for example, be interested in using a mapping application that supports data searches and user editing.

The public library is also a valuable resource to users who need assistance in map-related projects. From planning vacations, to downloading current mobile map or GPS applications, to accessing outline maps for school projects—these types of needs can easily be met with online map and GIS resources.

The Internet provides a gateway to a wide variety of maps and mapping platforms. Before WebGIS, some of the earlier online map resources were digital facsimiles or electronically created maps. The first classification of webmaps was made by Menno-Jan Kraak (2001), who distinguished between *static maps* and *dynamic maps*. These two categories were further subdivided into *interactive* and *view only* webmaps. Ten years later, we still have *view only* and *interactive* maps, but the interactivity features have expanded quite a bit since then. Today, many applications support user editing, sharing, and easy embedment in webpages and social network sites. The following sections examine the major types of map resources that are available online.

Static Digital Maps

Static digital maps, or electronic maps, are the digital equivalents of paper maps. They may consist of topographic maps, historical maps, country/city/road maps,

Figure 2.1. Search Results in Google (http://www.google.com/)

map my distance

About 77,100,000 results (0.15 seconds)

Map My Run ☆
... and running **maps** to measure **distance** and count calories from running. With running forums, training logs and tips from expert runners and coaches. ...
Login - Create Map - Running Routes - Search For Runs
www.**mapmyrun**.com/ - Cached - Similar

MapMyRun.com | Show Running Routes in Mountain View, Ca ☆
Running **maps**, **map** runs, running routes, running trails, jogging routes, ...
www.**mapmyrun**.com/search - Cached - Similar

⊞ Show more results from mapmyrun.com

Gmaps Pedometer ☆ - 2 visits - 27 Apr
running, **maps**, jogging, triathalon, biking, exercise, bikers, mileage, swimming, fitness, calorie counter, calculator, training, **distance**, running clubs, ...
www.**gmap**-pedometer.com/ - Cached - Similar

Google **Maps Distance** Calculator ☆
12 Aug 2010 ... By John on 05/11/2010 I love your valuable **distance** tool! I use it to **map** out long **distance** shortwave listening. This completes **my** ...
www.daftlogic.com › Projects - Cached - Similar

MapMyRide.com - **Map** your Cycling, Compete against Lance in the ... ☆
EventListings. Find An Event Submit an Event My Events ... Once your cycling **map** is complete you can quickly view it in 3D, satellite form, or share it with friends. ... Tags: Long **Distance**, Mostly on Bike Paths, Quiet, suburban ...
www.**mapmyride**.com/ - Cached - Similar

MapMyRide Community - calculating calories by **distance**, not time ☆
If I **map** a ride at 14 miles (yesterday's ride) but don't have **my** exact time ...
www.**mapmyride**.com/community/discussion/8888/ - Cached

⊞ Show more results from mapmyride.com

Measure **Distance** on a **Map** ☆
Take a measurement between two points on a **map** to find the **distance**. ... I LOVE THIS :D I could spend hours measuring **my distance**, I'm that sad :") ...
www.**freemaptools**.com/measure-**distance**.htm - Cached - Similar

Google **Map** Pedometer ☆
Calculate your route **distance** with this Google **map** pedometer. ... Measure Your Running Routes - **Map My** Run - iPhone **Maps** Direction Formats - iPhone Driving ...
walking.about.com/library/walk/blgooglemap1.htm - Cached - Similar

New Zealand runners, walkers and cyclists - **map** your routes ☆
New Zealand site to **map** and measure your sports routes. See how far you're going and track your ... Auto-follow roads. **Distance** markers. Auto-scroll **map** ...
nz.**mapometer**.com/ - New Zealand - Cached - Similar

Real-time GPS tracking for sports enthusiasts: **Map My** Tracks ... ☆
6 Sep 2010 ... New feature: Weekly summaries made easy for **distance**, duration, ... This is the blog of **Map My** Tracks, the easy way to accurately **map** or ...
www.**mapmytracks**.com/.../new-feature-weekly-summaries-made-easy-for-**distance**-duration-calories-and-activities/ - Cached

and thematic maps that are available for printing, viewing, or downloading in image format. Because these maps are static, they cannot be navigated (zoomed or panned), manipulated, or edited. Organizations such as historical societies, tourism bureaus, and map libraries often make maps available in this way. An example of an excellent collection of static maps is the University of Texas' Perry-Castañeda Library Map Collection (http://www.lib.utexas.edu/maps/index.html), which delivers access to static maps for the entire world.

More recently, organizations that host collections of map images on their websites opt to use web software that enables navigation ability. Offering interactivity to static images is limited, but it does offer users the ability to zoom, pan, or access more information via hyperlinks. Hyperlinking from a map or a map index has become quite popular among map collectors. The static map acts as an interface to additional images, maps, documents, or GIS data. The Brock University Map Library's 1921 Niagara Air Photo collection is an example of a map project that is accessed through static maps. When the user clicks on the desired area on the air photo index image (Figure 2.2), the user is led to the selected air photo (Figure 2.3).

Figure 2.2. Clickable Air Photo Index

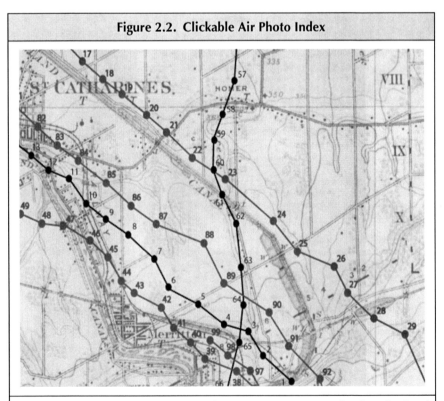

Source: Brock University Map Library, 1921 Air Photo Digitization Project, 2007; http://www.brocku.ca/maplibrary/airphoto/1921/1921_index.htm.

Figure 2.3. Selected Air Photo

Source: Brock University Map Library, 1921 Air Photo Digitization Project, 2007; http://www.brocku.ca/maplibrary/airphoto/1921/1921_index.htm.

Furthermore, the air photo, although static, has been enhanced with zoom and pan functionality using the HTML and flash-based product Zoomify. Although more information cannot be derived from this photo, using additional magnification technology like Zoomify provides users with access to and usability of high-resolution images.

Another popular navigational product used by map collectors is Luna Imaging software. Luna provides zoom and pan capabilities on images, and it organizes and catalogues the images accessible on the website. The David Rumsey Historical Map Collection (http://www.davidrumsey.com/) showcases scanned maps using Luna's

Zoomify

Zoomify is a tool used within webpages that makes images "zoomable." Zoomify takes the image and slices it into smaller tiles at varying sizes and resolutions. When users click on a section of the image, the individual "zoomed" tile is loaded and made available for viewing. Zoomify uses HTML, JPGs, and a Flash movie that serves as the "viewer." Zoomify Express is a free version of the product available for both Windows and Mac operating systems (Zoomify, 2010).

navigational support such as search, zoom, pan, and export. Figure 2.4 shows a digitized 1861 Civil War map available from the David Rumsey Historical Map Collection webpage (Cartography Associates, 2010). The image has a navigational bar that allows users to zoom into the image further. Figure 2.5 shows a

Figure 2.4. Digitized 1861 Civil War Map

Source: David Rumsey Map Collection; http://www.davidrumsey.com/.

Figure 2.5. A Portion of the Civil War Map Zoomed In

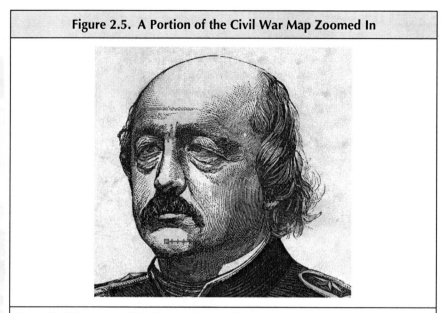

portion of the image that is zoomed in to its fullest extent. The ability to navigate and zoom into a static image offers users the type of detail that would be seen if they held a paper copy in their hands and looked through a magnifying glass.

Besides digitized scanned paper maps, there are also static maps available online that have been created electronically, using mapping programs. These types of maps often offer current sources of information for a wide range of themes. Some examples include the following:

- Crime Maps—Vancouver Police Department
  (http://vancouver.ca/police/crimemaps/index.htm)
- Statistical Maps—Statistics Canada Thematic Maps
  (http://geodepot.statcan.ca/Diss/Maps/ThematicMaps/index_e.cfm)
- Public Transit to School Maps—York Region Transit
  (http://www.yorkregiontransit.com/maps/yrt-to-schools.asp)
- U.S. National Parks—Terra Galleria Photography
  (http://www.terragalleria.com/parks/parks-map.html)
- Cemetery Maps—Norfolk County
  (http://www.norfolkcounty.ca/index.php?option=com_content&task=view&id=216&Itemid=17)
- Sightseeing Landmark Maps—City of New York
  (http://newyorkcity2005.web.infoseek.co.jp/information/sightseeing/landmark_m.html)

- Wind Power Maps—Southwest Windpower
  (http://www.windenergy.com/globalwindmaps/united_states.htm)
- Subway Maps—Amadeus Global Travel
  (http://www.amadeus.net/home/new/subwaymaps/en/)
- Organic Food Farms—*New York Times*
  (http://www.nytimes.com/imagepages/2009/05/03/business/
  03metrics.graf01.ready.html)
- Official Road Maps—Ontario Ministry of Transportation
  (http://www.mto.gov.on.ca/english/traveller/map/)
- Various Thematic and Topographic Maps—National Atlas of Canada
  (http://atlas.nrcan.gc.ca/site/english/maps/archives/5thedition)

Maps like the ones in this list can be found in a number of different ways. If a library client is asking about a specific resource, it's best to start with the source webpage (government or other organization website). Many organizations will have information available in a map format. Library websites tend to offer an excellent collection of links to maps. The University of Buffalo Library, for example, has an extensive list of map resources available at the local, state, and international levels (http://library.buffalo.edu/libraries/asl/maps/maps-gov-resources.html#usgsmaps). Alternatively, a Google search online with keywords such as "map," the geographic location of interest, and the theme will often provide results as well.

26

Basic Interactive Maps

In the past several years, map interactivity has become an expectation among many Internet users as they have become increasingly familiar with keyword location searches and navigational tools. The levels of map interactivity vary greatly, however, with some sites offering only navigational tools and others offering data imports and feature customizations.

Basic interactive maps are fairly simplistic maps created using online map making applications. These maps are often embedded into personal or organizational websites and often are a mashup of selected resources available from map applications. The basic interactive map will have a base map (i.e., background) composed of streets or aerial photography/satellite imagery that is available from Google Maps, Yahoo! Maps, Bing Maps, and other applications. However, in addition to simple navigational tools (zoom, pan), users can click on certain map features to gain additional information about them. Figure 2.6 is an example of a map that was created using Google Maps. It is available from the Greene County Public Library's webpage (http://www.greenelibrary.info/Collections-and-Resources/Cemeteries.html) and offers users a visual breakdown of township cemeteries in Greene County, Ohio. Clicking on any of the icons in the map will provide details on the location of the cemeteries.

Figure 2.6. Cemetery Map, Green County, Ohio

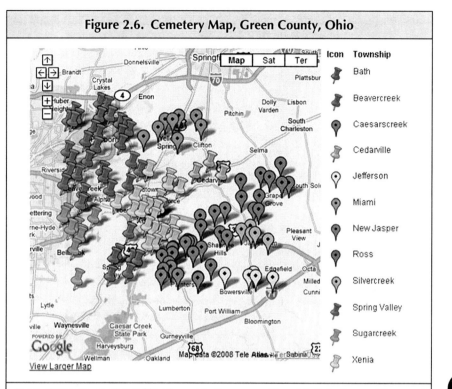

Source: Greene County (OH) Public Library; http://www.greenelibrary.info/Collections-and-Resources/Cemeteries.html.

27

Other maps provide basic interactivity to users, but they offer rather dynamic ways to search for information. Simple searches for geographic locations or directions exist in map sites like MapQuest (http://www.mapquest .com/) and Yahoo! Maps (http://maps.yahoo.com/), but searches for specific features are available in mashups that

> **Mashup**
>
> A mashup is an application or webpage that combines content from multiple webpages.

have been developed using a mapping application and at least one other online source of information. For example, the HousingMaps Website (http://www .housingmaps.com/) is a mashup using Google Maps and housing listings from Craigslist.

Millions of maps offer users interesting themes with search capabilities. Multiple Listing Services (MLS) (http://www.mls.ca/), for example, enables users to search for real estate based on specific criteria and then map the locations of all properties that meet the criteria. Flickr (http://www.flickr.com/map), a product by Yahoo!, maps the geotagged photos that users have contributed, thereby enabling photo searches based on location. Other popular mashups are those that offer current awareness. Those interested in the latest news can search for headlines based on geographic location. News Map (http://muti.co.za/static/newsmap .html) is one example of many that feeds its information from online news sites. The list of map themes available is endless: electoral maps, airport hotels, bike rentals, golf courses, top books, housing, and more. A comprehensive list is available from Programmable Web (http://www.programmableweb.com/api/google-maps/mashups).

Basic interactive maps offer users a visualization of specific features. The user can interact with the map by clicking on individual features and by conducting searches, but that's about it. Users can't change the look of the map—they can't customize the types of features or the appearances of them (symbols). Maps that offer customization, or personalization, further expand map interactivity, enabling users to select features to include on their map.

Personalized Interactive Maps

Personalized interactive maps are commonly created by businesses and organizations. A personalized mapping program enables users to somewhat customize the map by selecting from a list of available features. Unlike some of the maps mentioned previously, the features in this type of mapping program are not an all-or-none display of point features, but rather they may include several different types of map features such as points, lines, polygons, and images that can be independently activated on the map. With resources available across many sectors and discipline areas, this type of interactive mapping is an excellent source of information for library users.

Personalized interactive mapping programs are widely available across North America, often hosted by different levels of governments. Municipal maps are widely used by citizens and academics because of their localized source of information. Municipalities will often offer a large array of public services information in a map format—such as locations and information about municipal parks, facilities, and services. Some sites offer planning information like zoning, land use, waste disposal sites, and underground sewage. New York City offers an excellent visual gateway to the city's resources. Its mapping application consists of an interactive base map and aerial photographs of New York City, with additional clickable points of interest (http://gis.nyc.gov/doitt/nycitymap/). The features are categorized by government projects, city amenities, programs, cultural and educational institutions, municipal boundaries, service centers, and more. What makes this map personalized is that the user can add any listed individual feature to the map. Feature description is also available by clicking on its symbol on the map. Figure 2.7 shows a basic map without any of the features activated, and Figure 2.8 shows a more detailed version with additional features applied.

Once satisfied with the map, the user can save it, print it, and/or create a web link to the map. In save or print mode, the legend is automatically included, and

Figure 2.7. Basic Map without Features Activated

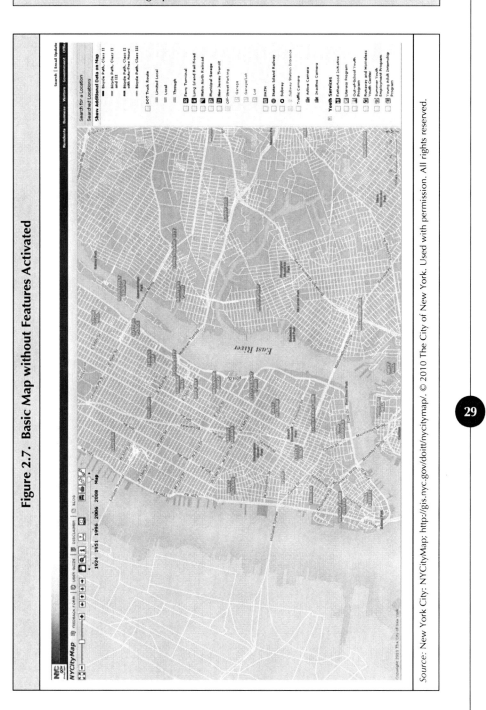

29

Figure 2.8. Map with Additional Features Activated

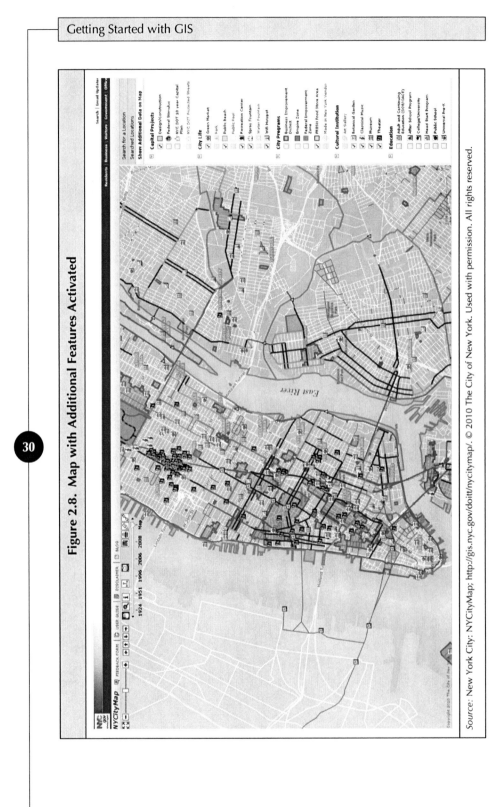

the user is prompted to add a map title. These hassle-free print features are what make map making so simple. With one click of a button, a customized map is generated and made available for sharing.

County level resources are also a rich source of municipal information. The County of Oxford, in Ontario offers an interactive map that focuses on planning (http://maps.county.oxford.on.ca/maps/landplan/viewer.html). Features that can be mapped include petroleum and water wells, waste disposal sites, sewage treatment plants, land use, zoning, vegetation, soils, and more. This site offers additional features to users such as querying (searching based on specific criteria), buffering (limiting features based on distance), and selecting specific features on the map. Users may find these features useful when searching for specific information within a distance radius.

There are some excellent provincial/state and national mapping resources available as well. Many offer topographic, hydrological, environmental, and geological information. Because of their cross-disciplinary themes, resources at this level of government prove to be very valuable to scholars. Most provinces and states in North America offer interactive mapping applications, and a large number of them offer their features for export or download. The data or features that are available for viewing may be exported and then used in a GIS program for further mapping. Even though these mapping applications offer user personalization and interactivity, some users are interested in further map customizations, as well as data analysis, that can be achieved only in a GIS software program. More and more applications are expanding the realm of mapping by offering an interface to meet the needs of map users of all levels.

Arguably one of the best sources for American national resources is the U.S. Geological Survey's (USGS) The National Map (http://nationalmap.gov/). The National Map is the product of a consortium of federal, state, and local partners, providing users with a wide range of applications from recreation to scientific analysis to emergency response. Maps can be created using the following data categories (USGS, 2010):

- Biology
- Boundaries
- Climatology/Climate Change
- Coastal Studies
- Digital Atlases
- Elevation
- Environmental Monitoring/ Assessment
- Geographic Names
- Geography
- Geology
- Gulf Coast Risk Assessment
- Hydrography
- Imagery
- Land Use/Land Cover
- National Grid
- Natural Hazards/Weather
- Public Land Records
- Structures
- Topographic Maps
- Transportation

31

The National Map offers something for everybody, as the disciplinary uses of this application are endless. The National Map provides more than a mapping viewer; it also provides access to data downloads, and it's considered to be a data distribution system as well. Users can specify geographic extents and individual datasets they would like downloaded. This type of mapping application is considered to be a geospatial portal because it provides one-stop access to maps, data, and more. Geospatial portals will be discussed further on in this chapter.

The National Map is a collaborative project, but it's certainly not the only one of its kind. There are many other governmental sources of information available. The U.S. Fish and Wildlife Service's (FWS) National Wetland Inventory (http://137.227.242.85/wetland/wetland.html) is one example that provides mapping information to the public on the status, extent, characteristics, and functions of wetland, riparian, deepwater, and other aquatic habitants (FWS, 2010). A large number of Ministries across North America provide their information freely to the public. Whether it's forestry, watershed, geology, soil, or meteorological information, scholars, particularly at the college and university levels, may find their applications very resourceful. Compiled lists of government mapping sites are available on the **companion website (http://www.neal-schuman.com/gis)**.

Editable Interactive Maps

The large number of maps that are available online are largely a product of the numerous map making applications that are made available to the general public. In the past few years, society's increased interest in creating customized maps has resulted in interactive mapping applications that offer user editing—that is, the ability to add personal data (like points of interest, images, and drawn shapes) to manipulate the overall look of the map. Editable interactive maps will often include features similar to those used in personalized maps, like preexisting features and a base map with streets or satellite imagery. However, the key difference is that editable mapping applications offer users the additional ability to add their own data, share their version of the map with others, and, with some applications, make it a permanent addition or change to the publically shared map.

Editable maps are just as easy to find and use as any of the other maps that have been mentioned. In fact, many readers will probably have some experience working with these maps already. One example is Google Earth, a virtual globe that has a large number of map-able themes. Users can activate any number of these themes; from historical maps, to natural and physical geography, to demographic statistics, Google Earth offers a bundle of resources for many disciplines to discover. Chapter 3 will go into more detail, including a thorough summary of Google Earth and its mapping tools. However, what's important to realize at this point is that users are not limited to learning about or using Google Earth's available features. The virtual globe is commonly used by educators, librarians, and students as a teaching and learning tool, a lightweight GIS application, and a customizable mapping program. Users can add information directly into the program by inserting placemarks, drawing shapes, and adding text and imagery.

One of the more advanced editing features is the ability to import geographic files in the Keyhole Markup Language (KML) format. This feature provides unlimited possibilities with map making and map sharing, as any GIS data, map, or image in KML format can be viewed in Google Earth. Some program converters available online will convert geographic files into the KML format that is required by Google Earth to display the geographic data.

Many data providers are now offering KML file downloads from their website. The Ministry of Northern Development, Mines and Forestry, for example, has created its own OGS (Ontario Geological Survey) Earth collection, providing users with geological maps in KML format. Figure 2.9 shows the OGS Earth

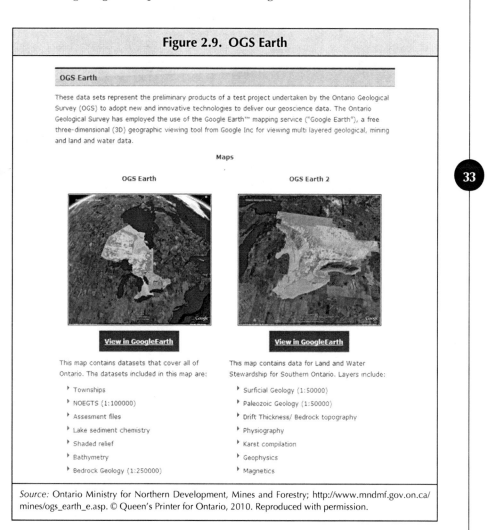

Figure 2.9. OGS Earth

OGS Earth

These data sets represent the preliminary products of a test project undertaken by the Ontario Geological Survey (OGS) to adopt new and innovative technologies to deliver our geoscience data. The Ontario Geological Survey has employed the use of the Google Earth™ mapping service ("Google Earth"), a free three-dimensional (3D) geographic viewing tool from Google Inc for viewing multi-layered geological, mining and land and water data.

Maps

OGS Earth

OGS Earth 2

View in GoogleEarth

View in GoogleEarth

This map contains datasets that cover all of Ontario. The datasets included in this map are:

▸ Townships
▸ NOEGTS (1:100000)
▸ Assesment files
▸ Lake sediment chemistry
▸ Shaded relief
▸ Bathymetry
▸ Bedrock Geology (1:250000)

This map contains data for Land and Water Stewardship for Southern Ontario. Layers include:

▸ Surficial Geology (1:50000)
▸ Paleozoic Geology (1:50000)
▸ Drift Thickness/ Bedrock topography
▸ Physiography
▸ Karst compilation
▸ Geophysics
▸ Magnetics

Source: Ontario Ministry for Northern Development, Mines and Forestry; http://www.mndmf.gov.on.ca/mines/ogs_earth_e.asp. © Queen's Printer for Ontario, 2010. Reproduced with permission.

33

Figure 2.10. OGS Earth KML File for Bedrock Geology (1:250,000) Displayed in Google Earth

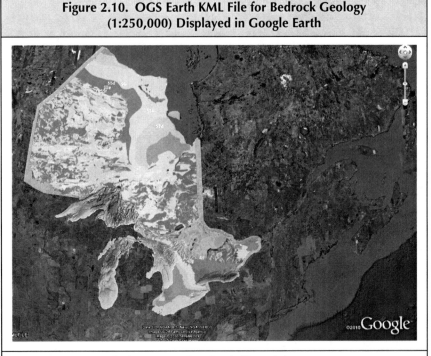

collection webpage. Figure 2.10 shows what the bedrock geology layer looks like when overlaid in Google Earth.

Google Earth's support for data imports makes an already dynamic application even more resourceful and applicable to a wider user base. Library professionals may find this to be the ultimate teaching tool in the classroom. With thousands of Google Earth–based teaching curricula available online for all levels and many subjects, library professionals will quickly realize the potential of teaching with GIS.

> **Keyhole Markup Language**
>
> Keyhole Markup Language (KML) was created by Keyhole, Inc., and acquired by Google in 2004. KML is an XML-based file format that describes geographic features using latitude and longitude coordinates. Popular examples of KML files include placemarks, images, text, and graphics (points, lines, polygons). KML is also available in its compressed zipped version, KMZ (*Wikipedia*, 2010a).

Many organizations and even some libraries are taking advantage of KML files' ease of use by making their own projects available in this file format. Anything that has a geographic component can be converted into a KML file, allowing the general public to work with geographic data without the need for sophisticated GIS software. Because Google Earth is a free downloadable install that is used by millions of people, it has become a popular medium to communicate information. KML files can be created in Google Earth as well and can easily be e-mailed to other users. Because of its popularity and practicality, it is a highly recommended program worth learning and teaching to library professionals and library users.

Google Earth is certainly not an exclusive user of KML and KMZ files. Several applications online support KML imports. The My Maps feature of Google Maps is one of them, additionally offering some basic map making features—although not nearly as dynamic as Google Earth's. Google Maps is also used to power other applications. Scribble Maps (http://www.scribblemaps.com/) is an online program that runs on Google Maps yet offers a completely different set of mapping tools. Users can add text, upload KML files, draw shapes, create markers, add images, and then share their completed map with others. With a click of a button, users can share their maps with friends on Facebook or obtain a widget code to embed into their webpages. Scribble Maps offers an easy way to add interactive maps into webpages. Figure 2.11 shows a map that was created in Scribble Maps. Figure 2.12 shows a Scribble Maps map that was embedded into a library webpage to show the location of the map library. Bing Maps is yet another application that offers similar features to those in Scribble Maps. These mapping applications will be discussed in more detail in Chapter 3.

Figure 2.11. Scribble Maps (http://www.scribblemaps.com/)

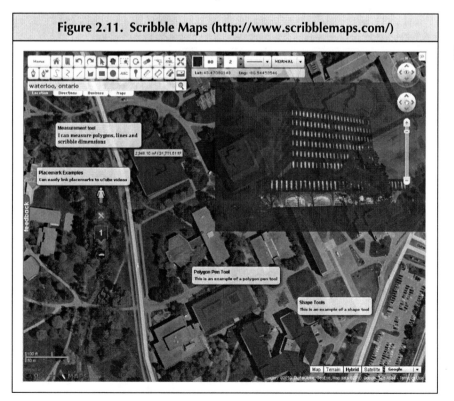

Figure 2.12. University of Waterloo Library's GIS Subject Guide with Embedded Map

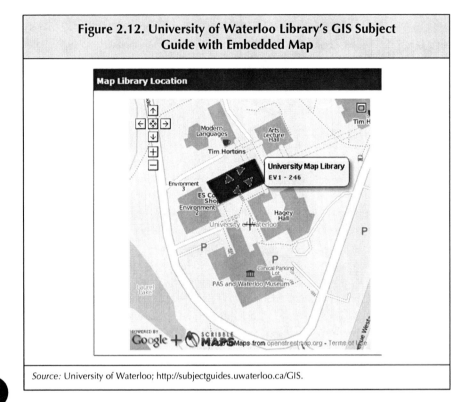

Source: University of Waterloo; http://subjectguides.uwaterloo.ca/GIS.

36

There are of course many other ways to customize a map besides importing KML files. A very simple, yet diverse use of a map is to view locations of points of interest. Some map users like to use the Placemark tool that is available in many applications, but spatially adding individual placemarks to known locations can be very time consuming. Users who have the information available in a table can simply import the table and view the locations as points. The table will need to include some geographic information such as street addresses or latitude and longitude coordinates. Some applications online will geocode the address information by adding columns to the table for latitude and longitude coordinates. All maps look for the coordinate information, so if the user doesn't have access to that (which is usually the case), it's important to know that there are tools online that will quickly and accurately translate addresses into geographic coordinates. This information can then be easily imported into an editable program such as Bing Maps, Scribble Maps, Google Earth, and so forth.

Geocoding addresses may be of interest to both library professionals and library users alike. Many libraries offer maps that showcase locations of a theme, such as library locations, book publishers, or library users. Students or other academics may wish to map themes that are related to their research—locations of survey respondents, locations of natural disasters (floods, fires, earthquakes), diseases, or perhaps commercialization and urban growth. Again, everything with a geographic location can be mapped, and it can be done so easily with the right tools.

BatchGeo (http://www.batchgeo.com/) is a free an online tool that geocodes addresses, maps them, and creates KML files for them. Tabular information is pasted into BatchGeo's webpage, and, in seconds, the tabular information is displayed in the website's interactive map. The user can also view the points in Google Earth. Figure 2.13 shows a BatchGeo screenshot after tabular data were processed.

A second tool that provides similar results is Community Walk (http://www.communitywalk.com/), an online mapping program powered by Google Maps. The user can enter a list of points with address information, and Community Walk will provide the coordinate information as well as display the results on a map. Community Walk is more of a mapping program than BatchGeo because it offers map making features as well.

There are plenty of online mapping tools available for people with varying interests to take advantage of. Everybody has an interest, and many people share similar ones. Thankfully, people's special interests and abilities to use online tools have developed into something that can be shared and used by all—hence the formation of citizen mapping, or volunteered geographic information (VGI). Instead of contributing toward a personal map, people can use applications that

Figure 2.13. BatchGeo Screenshot (http://www.batchgeo.com/)

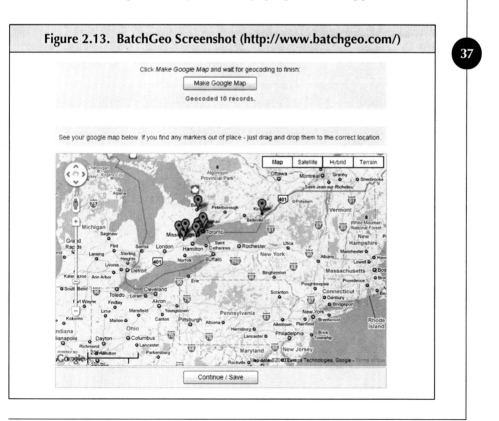

permit them to input and permanently save their information on a shared mapping platform. The knowledge set and information that every individual has is a great benefit to society, and VGI allows individuals to contribute their familiarity and awareness about places and spaces, making a permanent contribution for the rest of the world to use and learn from. Both amateurs and professionals contribute their geographic knowledge to applications that support VGI. These applications can be used for general information like points of interest, road and topography construction, and specialized neighborhood knowledge like species of trees grown.

Wikimapia (http://wikimapia.org/) is one example of an online application that relies on Internet users' contributions. Closely paralleling the *Wikipedia* project, people are invited to collaborate to improve information available on the Internet. Wikimapia is an online map resource that combines Google Maps with a wiki system that allows users to input information about any location on Earth. Contributors can add buildings, parks, lakes, bridges, settlements, roads, and rivers, and they can delete information that is inaccurate. Information can be added by drawing lines or polygons, adding informative tags, and permanently saving the information for the rest of Wikimapia users to see. As of December 2010, over 13,800,000 places were marked (*Wikipedia*, 2010c).

Maps that are based on information that has been contributed by members of society are often much more detailed than other maps available online. If library users are not inclined to contribute, they may be interested in using the map for topographic and cultural purposes. Figure 2.14 shows a landmark that was contributed by the author to Wikimapia.

Figure 2.14. Wikimapia Screenshot (http://wikimapia.org/)

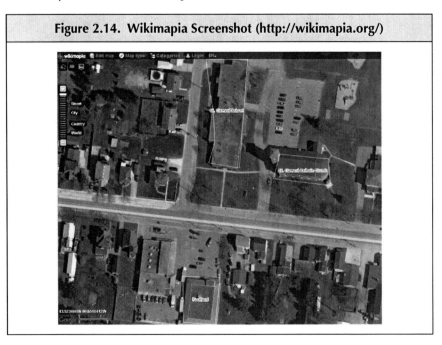

Another detailed and popular VGI project is OpenStreetMap (http://www.openstreetmap.org/), providing mapping information for the entire world. Internet users are invited to contribute their knowledge of geographic places by adding points of interest like parking, cafés, hotels, retail stores, telephones, fire stations, and more. Streets and rivers can be added and modified as well.

Users can also take advantage of the information that is available to them by viewing, creating maps, and even exporting the maps and data. OpenStreetMap is used by many as a very detailed topographical and cultural resource. As of November 2010, OpenStreetMap had 330,000 registered users (OpenStreetMap Wiki, 2010). Because of the large number of people involved in updating information, sites like these make an excellent resource for up-to-date maps. They are often used in emergency situations such as natural disaster rescue missions, where detailed maps are relied on to find victims and to begin rebuilding the community. The Haiti earthquake in January 2010, for example, prompted the OpenStreetMap community to collaborate their knowledge and efforts to build a comprehensive street map for Port-au-Prince. Without a post-disaster map available, one was essential to aid search and rescue missions. A new map was created almost immediately by tracing over satellite imagery showing critical features such as passable roads, hospitals, refugee camps, and cemeteries.

OpenStreetMap can be used in several applications. Scribble Maps, for example, offers a number of online base maps to select from. If users prefer to use OpenStreetMap street data over Bing satellite imagery, for example, they have the option to do so. Not all applications offer a choice in base map flavors, but those that do tend to include OpenStreetMap, Google, and Bing Maps. Using a specific map background to work with data available from other applications or mapping sites is a common feature in editable interactive mapping programs. In fact, users can build a wide range of thematic maps using just one application, where in the recent past they would have been required to visit multiple resources for the same information. The way this is accomplished is by creating maps that are being accessed from other mapping servers. The maps are requested by the user, generally by clicking on a button, and in return the user receives an image of the map or layers requested. The image will often draw on top of the base map in the current view. This type of service is called a Web Map Service (WMS).

Web Map Services expand the program's mapping capabilities by offering a large number of map layers to work with. ArcGIS Explorer Online (http://explorer.arcgis.com/) is an example of an excellent mapping application that offers 12 different base maps (streets, imagery, topographic, terrain and others), and a large amount of additional layers that can be added to the map. Specific themes can be searched across publicly shared maps, images, and feature services available from ArcGIS.com and other organizations that have freely opened up their layers to share with the world. Themes include demographics, elevation, topography, physical geography, and much more. ArcGIS.com is a repository of

39

Figure 2.15. ArcGIS Explorer Online (http://explorer.arcgis.com/)

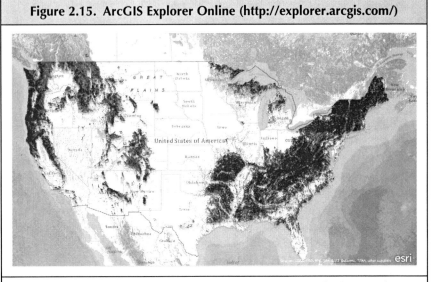

maps, data, tools, and applications that GIS users use to create and share maps. Maps that have been publically uploaded to this website are available for use by all ArcGIS.com and ArcGIS Explorer Online users. Figure 2.15 shows a screenshot of ArcGIS Explorer Online with additional USGS forestry landcover added via the WMS available through ArcGIS.com. This application will be discussed in more detail in Chapter 3.

Geospatial Portals and Data Repositories

A repository of maps, data, and tools such as ArcGIS.com is commonly considered to be a geospatial portal, or geoportal. Geoportals are websites that provide a single point of access to geospatial information that can be discovered, accessed, and used. Not only can users create maps and connect to data that belongs to a third party, but users can also download the data they are viewing. The downloads are typically available in a GIS format, enabling easy use in a GIS program or lightweight applications like Google Earth. For library users who are required to download GIS data, geoportals make it extremely convenient to do so.

Geoportals enhance information sharing by providing users with quick access to data, search tools, interactive mapping applications, and metadata. By having multiple resources available in one spot, portals offer an easier, faster, and less expensive GIS solution for all levels of government.

Geospatial One Stop (http://gos2.geodata.gov/wps/portal/gos) is an example of an American e-government initiative, managed by the Department of the Interior, that consists of a regional, national, and global portal that provides access to

WMS, downloadable data, and map making tools. Maps can be created with any of the following themes:

- Climate
- Conservation
- Environment
- Demography
- Federal Energy Activities
- Federal Lands
- Geology

- Hazards
- Human Geography
- Hydrology
- Topography
- Weather
- Wildfire

These numerous themes and more are available from contributing government agencies from the federal, state, local, and tribal levels, companies, academic institutions, nonprofit organizations, and individuals.

Geoportals offer Internet users collaborative projects that encourage government and nongovernmental organizations to share, organize, and distribute their resources. It also encourages users to take advantage of the information, as it is being offered to them in an easy-to-use fashion.

An excellent Canadian resource is GeoConnections (http://geodiscover.cgdi .ca/), covering a wealth of Canadian information at the national, regional, and provincial levels. The long list of themes available includes agriculture, biology, business, climate, environment, geology, utility, and much more. Users can download their data in a number of formats, including KML, and they can create a map using an updated interactive application. Figure 2.16 shows the GeoConnections mapping interface.

Figure 2.16. GeoConnections (http://www.geoconnections.org/)

Source: Reproduced with the permission of Natural Resources Canada, 2011.

Geoportals are a great place to begin looking for map resources, because they often represent many individual data providers. However, geoportals are not exclusive providers of data. Hundreds of thousands of other government and private websites individually offer their data for download. Although they may require some searching, these sites shouldn't be avoided. They are often the same ones that offer interactive mapping features and can be discovered via the respective government website or through a Google search.

The City of Vancouver (http://data.vancouver.ca/datacatalogue/) offers a phenomenal free data resource to the public. Its Open Data Catalog includes over 100 city-related layers, including bikeways, buildings, leash-free dog parks, schools, and election boundaries. The data are available in a number of formats, including the GIS shapefile (.shp), KML, Google Maps viewer, and Bing Maps viewer. As an example, users can easily download the KML files of interest and view the Vancouver data in Google Earth.

Of course not all government GIS projects offer their data in KML format, which arguably is one of the easiest ways for non-GIS experts to benefit from geographic information. Many times the data are in fact not accessible in a user-friendly format. Sometimes files may need to be converted, tables may need to be joined, and projections may need to be changed. The library user may need to find a GIS librarian or GIS expert for assistance with the more complex geographic files; however, overall, library professionals are encouraged to be aware of these types of data repositories. They may not always know how to work with the data, but being able to point users to a resource is a helpful step in the right direction.

Unfortunately, however, some of the resources that may be of interest to library users may not be freely available to them. Some data have a cost, and most municipal data, especially in Canada, are not accessible online because of data licensing restrictions. Many academic libraries do, however, have a GIS data collection that is accessible to many library users. The library professional may wish to become familiar with what is available in the library's holdings before spending time and effort searching for free data online. Data purchased and collected by the library are often available in a ready-to-use format and quite often are composed of more detailed information than what their online counterparts offer. The data are usually catalogued in some way, with descriptions available online as well. A compiled list of geoportals and websites that offer data for download is available on the **companion website (http://www.neal-schuman.com/gis)** a valuable resource to library users who inquire about map-able governmental resources.

Geosocial Networking and Mobile GIS

Society has become captivated by the ability to share where they are, where they are going, and where they have been. This has been made possible with technologies such as mobile devices, cameras, and social networking applications. It wasn't too long ago that the whereabouts of friends and family members weren't really that interesting. Now, people are not only tracking their friends and family, but they are willing to be tracked themselves, sharing in real time where they are located. Many mobile devices today have GPS chips, and, when combined with the right applications, users can provide instant location updates to their world of friends. Those who are looking for people to meet up with can just as easily track their location this way as well.

Several applications are currently being used for purposes of communicating whereabouts. Some networking applications will simply state the name of the location that users are presently at, and others will generate a map that will be automatically posted for them. The two most popular avenues for sharing geolocation statuses have always been Facebook and Twitter; however, more recently new geosocial networking applications have surfaced—namely, Foursquare, DoubleDutch, Gowalla, and Whrrl.

Geosocial networking doesn't require too many components. The user needs a GPS-enabled mobile device, such as an iPhone, Blackberry, Palm, or Android, an application that will allow the user to announce his or her locational positions, and friends or colleagues to share the information with.

Foursquare (http://foursquare.com/) is an example of a popular, innovative geosocial networking application that enables users to connect with "friends" by commenting on places and "checking in" to locations like bars, cafes, stores, and events. Foursquare has a competitive game and marketing component to it, whereby both Foursquare and certain businesses offer rewards for "checking in." Many organizations can of course take advantage of this type of development—providing rewards or incentives to visit the organization is one thing, but the amount of promotion the organization will get will result in arguably being the best avenue of promotion yet.

Professionals are also taking advantage of location and event check-ins in Foursquare by using the technology to connect at large events or gatherings, such as conferences. At large events, announcing arrivals to friends and colleagues may require several phone calls, but with geosocial networking applications like Foursquare, all contacts can be reached at once. As of September 2010, Foursquare had over 3 million users, adding around 15,000 users daily (Pandey, 2010).

Other mobile applications, like DoubleDutch and Gowalla, also offer check-ins, and many other geolocating applications allow users to announce their geographic positions. However, perhaps one of the more popular iPhone applications worth knowing about is one that is supported by Facebook. With over 500 million registered users, Facebook clearly is the leader in social networking technology. If a geosocial networking mobile application can reach Facebook users, then so many more "friends" are aware of the users' whereabouts.

Places is a new geolocation application for Facebook that allows check-ins through the iPhone. Users can share their location as well as tag friends who are accompanying them. Facebook has also partnered with Foursquare, Gowalla, and others and plans to incorporate their services into Places as well.

43

Several mapping applications online work with Facebook to post location or route updates. Map My Fitness (http://www.mapmyfitness.com/), Map My Ride (http://www.mapmyride.com/), Map My Walk (http://www.mapmywalk.com/), and others allow users to input their routes on a map and share their map on Facebook. Facebook also offers its own mapping applications that allow users to input places visited. The "Where I've Been" application allows users to create a map of all of the locations they have visited in the world. The map then gets installed on the user's profile page.

A map of all Facebook friends' locations is of course possible as well. Bing Maps has created an application called "My Friends," which pulls data from the user's Facebook account to geocode and map the locations of friends in Bing Maps. Seeing the locations of friends provides a different perspective of their whereabouts. Bing Maps also supports the social networking Twitter users. Users can create maps of tweets based on location or based on tweet themes. This may be useful for organizations that wish to embed a map on their website showing all local activity on Twitter that is relevant to their business.

Mobile devices provide a convenient and easy-to-use platform for sharing location information. Several applications can be synchronized with websites, but there are also many more standalone applications that are available for mobile devices as well. Because so many people today treat their iPhones, Blackberries, and iPods as mini-laptops, it's not surprising that there are mapping and GIS applications available to satisfy the needs of users on the go. From travelers, to GIS experts, there are several mobile applications to suit everybody's needs.

> **Twitter**
>
> Twitter is a social networking and microblogging website. Users can send and read messages, called "tweets," up to 140 characters in length. These messages are displayed on the user's profile page and displayed publically. A restricted list for friends is possible as well. Users can send and receive tweets online, which is compatible with many mobile devices (*Wikipedia*, 2010b).

Mobile GIS Applications

In the past few years, devices and applications like iPhones, Blackberries, and, more recently, Androids have almost completely replaced pocket and paper road maps. With several free mapping applications available now for mobile devices, people are using maps more than ever before. Mobile GIS applications, or mobile GIS, is a rapidly evolving GIS technology that offers users an easy and convenient way to collect and disseminate geospatial information. Locational information can be added into the application, with the additional ability for some devices to record video, record sound, and take pictures as well. With a simple click of a button, users instantly know where they are and how to get to their destinations, and they can share their adventures with their friends and colleagues.

One of the most popular mobile mapping applications is Google Maps for Mobile, with over 100 million users since August 2010 (Gundotra, 2010). Google Maps for Mobile has the following features:

- Navigation—Turn-by-turn GPS navigation with voice output (walking or driving)
- Place Finder—A searchable database of points of interest
- Driving Directions
- Transit Directions—Routes and schedules for subways and busses
- Biking Directions—Bike routes and trails
- Latitude—See friends' locations and share locations with them
- Traffic—Real-time information
- Street View—Street-level imagery

Google Maps for Mobile provides solutions for people needing daily routing assistance as well as for those who are traveling to unfamiliar places.

In lieu of a laptop computer, a phone or a Blackberry device can easily assist with navigational queries. Mobile applications are replacing the automobile GPS devices. For a fraction of the cost, users can use their phones and Blackberries as devices for personalized routes and directions. A study by comScore (2010) shows that the use of mobile devices for mapping applications has grown 44 percent between April 2009 and April 2010. In just the three months between January and April 2010 close to 33.35 million people in the United States used a map application from their mobile device. Nearly 87.2 percent utilize the mapping application while driving, 17.2 percent use it while walking/running or biking, and another 16.7 percent use it for public transit information. In fact, the use of social networking applications has jumped 240 percent in the one year, with map application usage increasing by 93 percent. Google Maps has been rated as the number three application downloaded for the iPhone, number two for the Blackberry, number one for the Android OS, and number two for all other smartphones (Tech Crunchies, 2010). The evidence clearly shows that mapping applications are being used by the general public, and, with public libraries receiving many directional and leisure-related locational reference questions, the following mobile applications are worth knowing about.

45

Trails

Trails is the first GPS iPhone application to record, import, and export tracks onto the iPhone. Using OpenStreetMap as the base map, users can record hiking, jogging, and biking routes and export the information in GPX format or to Google Earth. The application records speed, distance, and duration of tracks that can also be downloaded online. The application does not require an Internet connection (Lamouroux, 2008).

Topo Maps

Topo Maps is a viewer for U.S. Geological Survey (USGS) topographic maps and Canadian National Topographic System (NTS) topographic maps. With over 70,000 maps available, users can download any region of North America they would like. Searchable place names are also available with this application, as well as terrain data. The maps do not require an Internet connection, as the iPhone's GPS is used to track the user's location relative to the map (Endecott, 2010).

oMaps

oMaps is an offline application designed for travelers abroad who need international maps, but don't have easy (or affordable) Internet access. The maps need to be uploaded via the Internet before the user goes away. OpenStreetMap is the map source, and users are able to add placemarks on the map during their travels. This application is also compatible with the iPod Touch (Bonnin, 2009).

Serendipitor

Serendipitor provides users with an appreciation of the physical location. Instead of giving users the all too common shortest route map, this map application encourages its users to enjoy their travels and to find the time to enjoy suggested activities along the way. Serendipitor will provide a route to the user based on the amount of time the user has. Users are encouraged to take photos and share their serendipitous findings with their friends (Shepard, 2010).

46

ArcGIS

Users interested in features that are often found in online mapping sites can access similar features in GIS-based mobile applications. ArcGIS for iPhone is one example of a mobile GIS application that provides users with data available from ArcGIS Online, including WMS features, as well as support for user data inputs. The ArcGIS for iPhone application includes map navigation, search, identify, and measure tools; WMS; and GIS analysis. ArcGIS for Mobile is certainly more common with GIS users than with the general public; however, it's important to point out the different levels of sophistication that exist in mapping applications.

Using GIS Technology in Libraries

This chapter has focused on introducing the reader to a large number of mapping resources that are available online. If a library user has a need for a map, then the library professional will have enough familiarity with the recourses available to help guide the library user in the right direction. However, providing reference or information services is not always so straightforward; many times library users don't know what it is that they need. They know what they want, but often they are unsure how to ask the questions that will connect them to the relevant resources. Library professionals need to take the perspective of the library users and anticipate what their needs and solutions may be. The library professional needs to be well rehearsed in the resources that are available in order to recommend a particular direction for the user's specific needs.

In academic libraries, subject librarians are specialized in certain subject matters and will often have enough of a background in the subject that they can assist library users by recommending appropriate and related resources that the library user may not be familiar with. Because maps and GIS are multidisciplinary subjects, it is recommended that all subject librarians learn about the mapping resources that pertain to their subject fields. The same of course can be said for public library professionals. Because they often cater to elementary and high school students, and adults from different backgrounds and with varying interests, they too need to be well informed about mapping resources that pertain to all subjects and themes—especially because a map may be a resource that the library user had not considered. This section will discuss some of the subjects and users who may be interested in the online mapping applications that have been discussed so far in this chapter.

Simple Mapping with Online Applications

Mapping resources are a rich source of information about land and people. Any map that offers aerial photography, both historical and current, coupled with topographic and cultural features can provide a great deal of information. Google Earth is an example of an exceptional resource for all grade levels, providing information on a wide range of themes. For example, society and culture can be analyzed by studying photographs that are available from the Street View and 360Cities panoramic imagery, as well as the user-submitted photograph collection that continues to grow daily. Photography provides information on countries and cities that many will never have a chance to visit themselves. Analyzing the city's infrastructure, transit system, citizens' styles of clothing, and how people occupy their time can be done with Google's photography collection.

Google Earth's aerial photography and satellite imagery are particularly helpful resources, because imagery is available for many areas of the world for more than one period. Historical aerial photographs can be compared with other years to analyze change in land over time. Whether it's to study land development growth and deforestation, to analyze damage from a natural disaster, or to observe changes in individual properties, aerial photography is used by many scholars as a reliable record of the past and present. Aerial photography is also very popular among archaeologists, genealogists, land developers, planners, environmentalists, and naturalists. Google Earth has been used by researchers to discover archaeological remains (Butler, 2005), new species of animal and plant life (Gray, 2008), human fossils (Van Grove, 2010), and meteor craters (Watts, 2010).

The ability to access KML files from many government websites and view them in Google Earth expands Google's usage across even more

47

subjects—climatology, geology, health studies, statistics, demographics, politics, and so on. Because most subjects can be mapped, many students, researchers, and teachers will find resources of interest to them.

As mentioned earlier, Google Earth makes a very dynamic and interactive teaching tool. Not only do instructors use the virtual globe to teach spatial literacy, but they also use it as a presentation tool and mapping program. Because users can add their own information into the program, Google Earth can easily be transformed into a customized application for the classroom. Similar concepts are found in ArcGIS Explorer Online, where the program has a built-in presentation builder. Any topic that has a connection to a location can be mapped and captured in a dynamic "playback" presentation. This is a popular feature among elementary school and high school teachers.

Online mapping applications that offer lightweight mapping tools allow researchers and scholars the ability to visualize and present their research findings. Bing Maps, Google Maps, Yahoo! Maps, and so forth, all offer simple business searches, making them ideal platforms for those needing to work with any projects related to business locations. The mapping tools essentially allow any landmark to be discovered and any feature to be added to the map, expanding the list of uses even more.

Interactive websites offer a great deal of information to planners, geographers, environmentalists, as well as to local residents. As discussed earlier, municipal sites offer information on city services, individual properties, parks and green spaces, rivers and lakes, and neighborhood-level information such as house values and tax assessments. Local information is also available from historical and genealogical societies, where they have geotagged or georeferenced historical photos and documents. Those with their own personal historical collections may wish to take advantage of digitizing and georeferencing or geotagging their documents as well.

In addition to academic uses, there are many resources of interest for personal purposes. As discussed earlier, many people take advantage of locational applications for socializing, networking, and communicating with others. Vacationers and travelers, for example, may wish to download some maps to help aid in navigation, such as topographic maps, road maps, GPS maps, and of course map applications for mobile devices. Upon their return from a trip, they may wish to take advantage of geotagging their photos, or re-creating their trip route in a map format.

Library professionals can significantly increase exposure to their library's collection and services with mapping and GIS resources. Collections can be digitized and presented online; library services and events can be promoted using locational applications; and information and instruction services can be advanced to include the latest cutting edge GIS technology and resources.

The ways novice GIS users can incorporate GIS into their daily lives is surprisingly easy. Millions of people are using it because GIS has evolved into a multidisciplinary user-friendly technology. GIS technology offers solutions for both simple and complex problems, with the more complex ones often being used by GIS professionals and experts who use GIS technology to analyze spatial relationships for problem solving and decision making.

Advanced uses of GIS have not been discussed in this chapter because most library users will not inquire about assistance with some of the more complex GIS concepts and associated software training. Library professionals are also not required to have advanced skills in GIS. Inquiries about GIS software, GIS data, and related theoretical concepts are subject specific and are often forwarded to the GIS or Map Librarian. Academic libraries will see more of these types of requests than public libraries. The next section will introduce the reader to some of the ways that expert GIS users utilize GIS technology.

Advanced Uses of GIS

GIS is used in academic institutions in a couple of different ways. First, GIS is a subject and is taught in GIS courses. Students gain an understanding of GIS principles and theories along with hands-on technical experience with desktop GIS software. Second, GIS is a technology that is used across several disciplines to help make decisions and solve problems within those disciplines. GIS is used by students and faculty in geography, planning, environmental resource studies, engineering, architecture, earth sciences, and others. Subject librarians at academic libraries may find it helpful to learn a bit more about how GIS is used in their subjects.

Some examples of GIS usage include determining prime locations for new establishments (business, highway, wind farm), analyzing multiple variables for cause and effect relationships, and studying environmental changes over time (erosion, water depth, deforestation) to name a few. Students may require assistance from the map or GIS librarian to access the GIS data they need, as well as to receive technical assistance using the software program.

GIS is used in practically all sectors of society. It is used as a tool to assist and manage in marketing, public health, natural resources, emergency management, transportation, and natural disaster predictions. We have already seen how government organizations use GIS to store, display, and disseminate data and maps to the public through interactive mapping applications. But government organizations also use GIS to organize, update, visualize, and analyze information such as economic development (from personal properties to newly installed utility lines), census surveys, emergency response plans, law enforcement (crime fighting), health care management, infrastructure management (e.g., transportation) and much more (Esri, 2010).

Businesses are prime users of GIS as well, especially for targeting current and potential customers. GIS can reveal the locations of customers, their demographic characteristics, and their spending patterns. GIS can also assist businesses in tracking competition, as well as to determine best locations for additional

49

businesses. This type of information can help businesses make decisions about products and inventory, methods of advertising, and which products to advertise, as well as gain insight into what the community's commodity needs are.

One of the larger sectors that relies on GIS technology is the natural resources. GIS is a powerful tool that helps manage many of the Earth's resources, such as agriculture, forestry, and petroleum. Within agriculture, GIS helps manage healthy growth and production of agricultural crops. The ability to record soil and irrigation conditions, plant health, and pest occurrences using mobile GIS devices allows for accurate study and improvements of agricultural processes. Likewise, the forestry industry takes advantage of GIS technology to monitor the health of trees, maintain timber inventories, analyze areas that require regeneration, and so forth. One final example is the use of GIS in the petroleum industry. GIS is used to determine the best location to drill a well, to route a pipeline, to build a refinery, and finally to reclaim a site (Esri, 2010). There are many more examples of GIS being used within dozens of industries. Esri (http://www.esri .com/industries.html) does a fabulous job summarizing the role of GIS in industry.

Conclusion

GIS is a multidisciplinary tool used for visualization, management, storage, and analysis of information. GIS is a powerful aid in helping students and professionals solve problems and find answers to questions. GIS has become a permanent part of society, making an impact on organizations and individuals on a daily basis. Today, GIS involves and includes everybody—both expert and novice users. Through user-friendly interfaces, all members of society can interact with information that is presented in a visual format. This ease of use has finally bridged the gap between GIS users and non-GIS users.

Chapter 3 will provide readers with an opportunity to explore the online world of mapping. Several tutorials have been created to guide readers step by step toward online map creation. Chapter 4 will lead the user into more advanced mapping, using GIS software applications for the purposes of customized mapping and simple spatial analysis.

References

Bonnin, Thomas. 2009. "oMaps: Official Maps for iPhone." Thomas Bonnin. http:// omapsiphone.com/.

Brock University. 2007. "1921 Air Photo Digitization Project." Brock University Map Library. http://www.brocku.ca/maplibrary/airphoto/1921/1921_index.htm.

Butler, Declan. 2005. "Enthusiast Uses Google to Reveal Roman Ruins." *Nature News*, September 14. http://www.nature.com/news/2005/050912/full/news050912-6.html.

Cartography Associates. 2010. "David Rumsey Map Collection." Cartography Associates. http://www.davidrumsey.com/.

comScore. 2010. "Apps for Maps: Smartphones Drive Gains in U.S. Mobile Navigation." comScore, Inc. http://www.comscore.com/Press_Events/Press_Releases/2010/6/ Apps_for_Maps_Smartphones_Drive_Gains_in_U.S._Mobile_Navigation.

Endecott, Philip. 2010. "Topo Maps." Philip Endecott. http://topomapsapp.com/guide_welcome.html.

Esri. 2010. "Esri Industries: GIS Mapping Solutions for Industry." Esri. http://www.esri.com/industries.html.

Felberbaum, Michael. 2010. "Companies Yank Cord on Residential Phone Books." *My Way News*, November 11. http://apnews.myway.com/article/20101111/D9JE3TG00.html.

FWS (Fish and Wildlife Service). 2010. "Wetlands Product Summary." U.S. Fish and Wildlife Service, National Wetlands Inventory. Last modified September 30. http://www.fws.gov/wetlands/Data/Products.html.

Gray, Louise. 2008. "Scientists Discover New Forest with Undiscovered Species on Google Earth." *Telegraph*, December 21. http://www.telegraph.co.uk/earth/earthnews/3884623/Scientists-discover-new-forest-with-undiscovered-species-on-Google-Earth.html.

Gundotra, Vic. 2010. "To 100 Million and Beyond with Google Maps for Mobile." *Google Mobile Blog*, August 19. http://googlemobile.blogspot.com/2010/08/to-100-million-and-beyond-with-google.html.

Kraak, Menno-Jan (ed.). 2001. "Settings and Needs for Web Cartography." In *Web Cartography*, edited by Menno-Jan Kraak and Allan Brown, 3–4. New York: Taylor and Francis.

Lamouroux, Felix. 2008. "Trails: Intuitive GPS Tracking on the iPhone." Felix Lamouroux. http://trails.lamouroux.de/.

OpenStreetMap Wiki. 2010. "Stats." OpenStreetMap Wiki, November 4. http://wiki.openstreetmap.org/wiki/Stats#OpenStreetMap_Statistics_Available.

Pandey, Shailendra. 2010. "Foursquare Passes 3M Users, For How Long Will It Resist Acquisitions?" Telecoms, September 27. http://www.telecoms.com/22563/foursquare-passes-3m-users-for-how-long-will-it-resist-acquisition/.

Shepard, Mark. 2010. "Serendipitor." Mark Shepard. Accessed December 21. http://www.serendipitor.net/.

Tech Crunchies. 2010. "Most Popular Mobile Applications." Tech Crunchies. http://gorumors.com/crunchies/most-popular-mobile-apps/.

USGS. 2010. "The National Map." U.S. Geological Survey. Last modified December 3. http://nationalmap.gov/.

Van Grove, Jennifer. 2010. "Google Earth Helps Scientists Discover New Species of Early Man." Mashable. http://mashable.com/2010/04/08/google-earth-sediba/.

Watts, Anthony. 2010. "Google Earth Leads to Spectacular Meteor Crater Find." *Watts Up with That* (blog), September 24. http://wattsupwiththat.com/2010/09/24/google-earth-leads-to-spectacular-meteor-crater-find/.

Wikipedia. 2010a. "Keyhole Markup Language." *Wikipedia*. Last modified November 10. http://en.wikipedia.org/wiki/Keyhole_Markup_Language.

———. 2010b. "Twitter." *Wikipedia*. Last modified December 19. http://en.wikipedia.org/wiki/Twitter.

———. 2010c. "Wikimapia." *Wikipedia*. Last modified December 18. http://en.wikipedia.org/wiki/WikiMapia#cite_note-4.

Zoomify. 2010. "Zoomify—Zoomable Web Images!" Zoomify, Inc. http://www.zoomify.com/.

A Guide to Web Mapping Applications: Hands-On Tutorials

Introduction: Online Mapping Application Tutorials

This chapter is composed of training material that will guide the reader into developing working knowledge of some of the more relevant online map applications applicable to libraries and their users. With the exception of Google Earth, all applications are available online and do not require any software downloads. However, some will require the creation of user accounts. The following self-paced tutorials have been written to familiarize readers with the general concept of interactive mapping programs, as well as to become a fluent user of specific programs. Readers may find these guides useful in their reference work, library projects, for teaching, as well as using them for training programs. The guides include American FactFinder, Region of Waterloo GIS Locator, Google Earth, Scribble Maps Pro, Google Maps, and OpenStreet-Map. Other popular mapping applications are discussed in Chapter 5, where the tutorials are for specific library-related projects. After completion of the tutorials in this chapter, readers will have a solid background in online mapping, being able to create personalized maps, understand how other online maps have been created, become proficient in popular programs like Google Earth, learn how to embed a map into a webpage, and know which resources to point library users to.

Interactive Government Mapping Applications

Interactive mapping applications that are most resourceful to library users are either topic specific or location based, such as local information discovered through municipal level government applications. As discussed in Chapter 2, specific themes can be found online by going directly to the source's webpage or by performing keyword Google searches. The interactive applications

53

will of course vary in information provided, but the technical concepts are all similar. All applications will have a main mapping page where the map is drawn. There will be typical navigational tools, as well as a list of layers to choose from. A legend will describe the symbols depicted on the map. Users will be able to print or save the map, and, depending on the site's copyright policy, they may share their customized map with others and/or link to it from a webpage.

Where applications tend to differ from one another is with some of the more advanced features offered. For example, some applications offer layer searches, queries, buffers, distance measurements, and a range of customizable map making tools. Users will need to explore the program on their own to learn its limitations. All applications will have a Help section that will summarize the features available.

To help users become familiar with the look and feel of standard interactive mapping applications, applications will be examined from two levels of government, national and municipal: the U.S. Census Bureau American FactFinder and the Region of Waterloo GIS Locator.

U.S. Census Bureau American FactFinder

American FactFinder (http://factfinder.census.gov/) is an interactive database from the U.S. Census Bureau that offers historical and projected census data for viewing and for download. Data available include population, housing, and business statistics in the form of maps, tables, and reports. Although the website is primarily a vehicle for distributing census data, it also provides a mapping application to view thematic maps for the 2000 Census, the 1990 Census, the Economic Census, and the Population Estimates program. With this program, the user can compare statistical data, analyze patterns, and customize the map's display by manipulating the class ranges and colors.

Getting Started

Note: A new version of American FactFinder will be released in the future. An updated tutorial will be made available on the **companion website (http://www.neal-schuman.com/gis)**.

Go to the American FactFinder website (http://factfinder.census.gov/). The left-hand side connects the user to the data, reports, and maps available from the Census Bureau. Near the bottom of the list, click on **Maps** (Figure 3.1).

Two different map types are available. One is a reference map that will display census boundaries, and the second is a thematic map that will display the census data. We are interested in the thematic map type. Select **Thematic Maps (data)**.

Figure 3.1. American FactFinder Main Page

Source: U.S. Census Bureau, American FactFinder; http://factfinder.census.gov/.

Some of the most popular map themes are listed under the categories of People, Housing, Business, and Government. These maps provide information at the state geography level. To access a thematic map on any of these topics, simply click on the link of interest to open the map. More maps are also available from the left menu, under each of the three categories. Click on **Percent of People below Poverty Level 2009**, under the People category. This theme will now display in a map format (Figure 3.2).

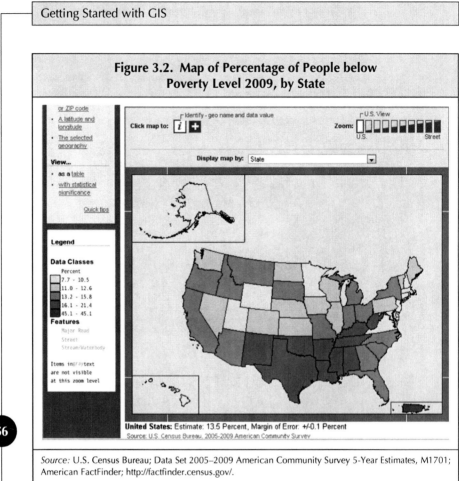

Figure 3.2. Map of Percentage of People below Poverty Level 2009, by State

Source: U.S. Census Bureau; Data Set 2005–2009 American Community Survey 5-Year Estimates, M1701; American FactFinder; http://factfinder.census.gov/.

This map application offers zoom and pan navigation, individual state attribute information via the Identify tool, and a legend with a default classification and color scheme. The user can change the class range of values, as well as the map colors. The user can also zoom into a specific geographical area by entering address information or geographic coordinates.

Zooming into a Specific Location

In the top-left section of the page, under **Reposition on ...**, click on **A street address or Zip Code**. Type in the address **Inwood Hill Park**, and Zip Code **10034**. Click on **Go**. The map will zoom into Inwood Hill Park in New York City. You will notice that street names are available at this local level. Additional map features are also available and need to be activated to view them.

Changing Map Content

The user can customize the map to include additional features, as well as change the thematic class ranges and colors. In the top-left section of the page, under **Change …**, click on **Data Classes**. Four folders are available: Classes, Boundaries, Features, and Title. You will be adding additional features to your map first. Click on the **Features** folder, and activate all of the features available in the list (Figure 3.3). Click on **Update**.

The list of features has been added to the map, as well as to the legend on the left side of the page. Feel free to navigate the map by zooming in and out to get a feel for the type of detail available. When you're done with that, zoom all the way out to the U.S. View zoom level.

Now you're going to change the classification method and color scheme of your map. Take a close look at the legend that is symbolizing percentage of population below poverty level. The default classification method is Natural Class Breaks. If you prefer a different distribution of numbers, you can change the classification in the **Classes** folder under **Change …**, **Data Classes**. Go to this folder now and change the Classing Method to **Equal Interval**. Feel free to change the color scheme at this point as well, if you wish. Update the changes and analyze how your map has changed. It is important to understand that maps can be manipulated to show different information very easily just by changing the class breaks and class methods.

Figure 3.3. List of American FactFinder Features Available for Activation

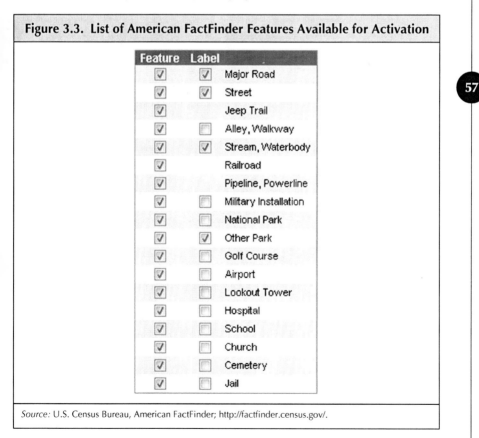

Source: U.S. Census Bureau, American FactFinder; http://factfinder.census.gov/.

Last, add a title to your map. Click on the **Title** folder, again in the **Data Classes** window. Give your map an appropriate title, and update the changes.

Saving and Printing

Near the top of the page, the **Print/Download** tab allows users to save and print the map, along with the legend and data information. The final map can be saved in PDF format. Users also have the option to download the tabular data that is associated with the specific census theme selected.

Other Themes and Levels of Geography

The map you have just looked at was selected from the popular list available on the main page. There are of course many more themes available and at different levels of geography. If you go back to the main thematic map page (http://factfinder.census.gov/) and, on the left-side panel, click on **Maps**, and then **Thematic Maps**, you will see a hyperlink to **Data Sets with Thematic Maps** (Figure 3.4). Clicking on this link will send you to a much larger data bank to work with. Click on the first data set, the **Census 2000 Summary File**, and click on **Next**.

58

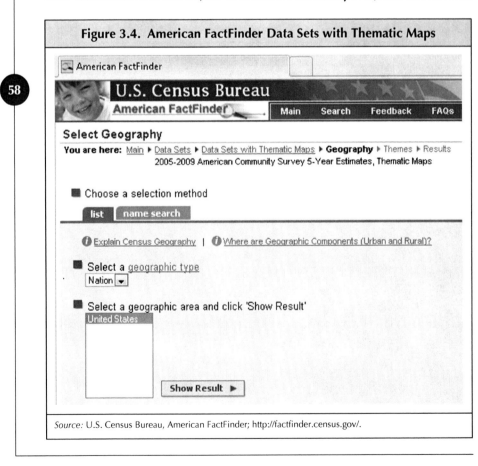

Figure 3.4. American FactFinder Data Sets with Thematic Maps

Source: U.S. Census Bureau, American FactFinder; http://factfinder.census.gov/.

The first step is to select the geography level of interest. The user can specify the geographic type (national, regional, divisional, urban area, etc.) as well as the geographic location of interest. Under **Geographic Type**, select **Urban Area**, and then under **Geographic Area** select **Miami, FL Urbanized Area** (Figure 3.5). Because of the large number of data sets available for Urban Areas, it may take the Geographic Area table some time to load.

Click **Next** to select a theme to map. Ensure that the **By Subject** folder is selected. Select a subject and then a theme that you are interested in. Click on **Show Results** to build your map. You can now customize your map further if you wish. You may want to spend some time familiarizing yourself with the large number of data sets available through American FactFinder.

Interested in Other Census Products?

Several mapping programs are available that can be used to create maps from census data. Many are available online and are often subscribed to by university, college, and public libraries. Social Explorer (http://www.socialexplorer.com/) is a reference tool for current and historical American census data from 1790 to present, offering users a wide number of variables and geographic locations to map. SimplyMap (http://www.simplymap.com/) is available for American and Canadian censuses, offering more complex map creations. A tutorial for SimplyMap is available from the **companion website (http://www.neal-schuman.com/ gis)**. One final program worth looking at is '*The New York Times*' Mapping America (http:// projects.nytimes.com/census/2010/explorer), a free online application that provides local American census data based on limited samples from the 2005 to 2009 Census Bureau's American Community Survey.

59

Figure 3.5. Selecting the Geography Level for the Census 2000 Summary Data Set

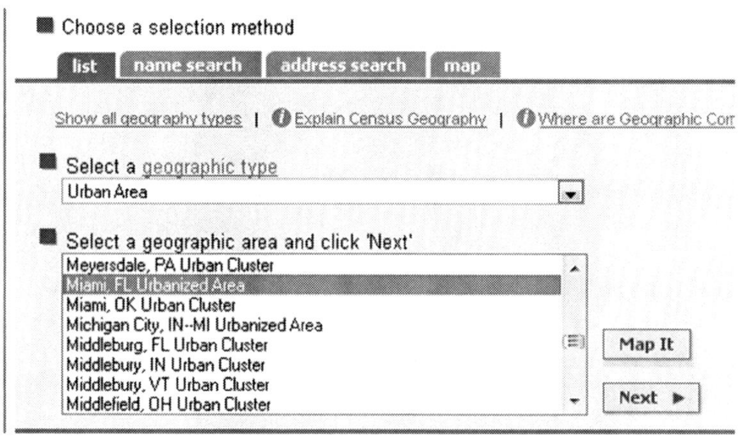

■ Choose a selection method

| list | name search | address search | map |

Show all geography types | ⓘ Explain Census Geography | ⓘ Where are Geographic Com

■ Select a geographic type

Urban Area ▾

■ Select a geographic area and click 'Next'

Meyersdale, PA Urban Cluster
Miami, FL Urbanized Area
Miami, OK Urban Cluster
Michigan City, IN--MI Urbanized Area
Middleburg, FL Urban Cluster
Middlebury, IN Urban Cluster
Middlebury, VT Urban Cluster
Middlefield, OH Urban Cluster

Map It

Next ▶

Source: U.S. Census Bureau, American FactFinder; http://factfinder.census.gov/.

Region of Waterloo GIS Locator

Municipal level interactive map applications are available for most large cities and many smaller ones in both the United States and Canada. As mentioned in Chapter 2, municipal level mapping applications often consist of topographic and recreational information available at the regional or city level. Municipal maps often provide users with the locations of trails, parks, wooded areas, streams, lakes and rivers, landmarks such as historical sites and government buildings, public services such as hospitals and religious organizations, and so forth. In addition to natural and cultural features, municipal maps tend to also include property parcel information, which may interest current or potential home owners, planners, developers, genealogists, and the like. Additionally, municipal level maps often offer region or citywide aerial photography. Of course every city offers its own flavor of data, but it is becoming common to see aerial photography reflecting a number of different years, allowing users to compare and contrast changes in the city's development.

A municipal level application that has been around for a number of years and offers many of the features mentioned earlier is the Region of Waterloo GIS Locator (http://maps.region.waterloo.on.ca/locator/locator.htm). In this tutorial, you will use this application to become familiar with the concept of municipal mapping. Note that the Locator works best with Microsoft's Internet Explorer (IE).

60

About the Locator

The Region of Waterloo Locator has been providing topographical, recreational, and cultural information and aerial photography to the public for ten years. It offers an easy to use interface that provides the locations of and information for a large number of features within the Region of Waterloo, including these:

- Landmarks
  - Government Buildings
  - Historical Sites
  - Regional Airports
- Public Services
  - Religious Organizations
  - Medical Services
  - Educational Institutions
  - Other Groups and Associations (daycares, community centers, cultural associations, etc.)
- Points of Interest
  - Historical and Heritage
  - Sports & Recreation
  - Lodging
  - Arts
  - Entertainment
- Streets
  - Provincial Highways
  - Regional Roads
  - Municipal Roads
- Parcels (property)
  - Parcel Address
  - Parcel Roll Number

- ○ Property Category
- ○ Survey Description
- ○ Acreage Size
- Aerial Photography
  - ○ 1993—1 m resolution, Region wide
  - ○ 2000—10 cm resolution, TriCity; 30 cm resolution, Region wide
- ○ 2003—10 cm resolution, Urban areas
- ○ 2006—30 cm resolution, Region wide
- ○ 2009—10 cm resolution, Urban areas

The GIS Locator offers several tools for users to effectively locate and display municipal features on the map. Users can specifically search and query for individual items from the categories listed. Users can also create buffers, select objects, measure, add text, add imagery, and adjust the scale. You'll learn more about these tools in the upcoming sections.

Getting Started

Go to the Region of Waterloo GIS Locator website (http://maps.region.waterloo .on.ca/locator/locator.htm), and read the Terms and Conditions available on the left panel. To begin, explore the Menu tools at the top of the page. Click on **Query** and then **Points of Interest** to begin searching the database (Figure 3.6).

On the left-side panel, the Points of Interest Query page pop ups. In this tutorial, you are interested in locating recreational facilities in the Region of Waterloo. Under **Type**, select **Sports & Recreation**. Under **Category**, select **Recreation Facility**. Under **Name**, all of the recreation facilities will be listed. You now know of all of the recreation facilities available in the Region of Waterloo. Select **YMCA of Kitchener-Waterloo** (Figure 3.7).

Click on the link to zoom into the YMCA. You may also notice that below the link you can also search for any point of interest by name. If you happen to lose the location of the YMCA, you can simply type it in the search field without having to perform the same type of query search. The map has now zoomed into the vicinity of the YMCA, with the facility being labeled and symbolized by a red pushpin. To find out all the features available on this map, view the list of layers. From the top Menu, select **View**, **Layer List**.

61

Figure 3.6. ROW GIS Locator Menu Tools

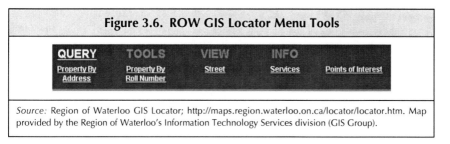

Source: Region of Waterloo GIS Locator; http://maps.region.waterloo.on.ca/locator/locator.htm. Map provided by the Region of Waterloo's Information Technology Services division (GIS Group).

Figure 3.7. Points of Interest Query in ROW GIS Locator

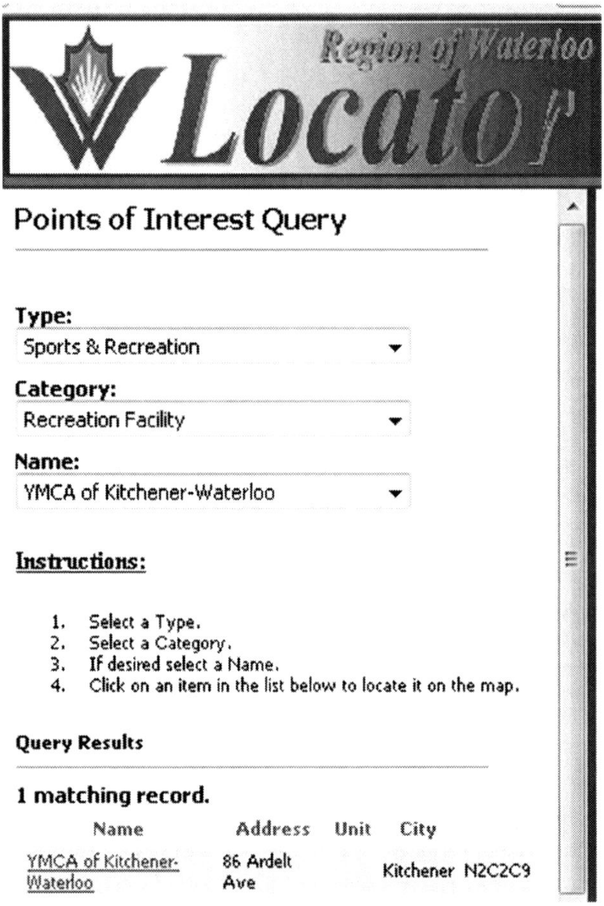

Source: Region of Waterloo GIS Locator; http://maps.region.waterloo.on.ca/locator/locator.htm. Map provided by the Region of Waterloo's Information Technology Services division (GIS Group).

You will now have a list of all the layers that are visible to you at this level of scale. Examine the list of layers to get a sense of the types of features that can be mapped. You will notice that in the Visible column, only a few layers are selected. You can make all or some of the layers visible by selecting them and then clicking on the **Refresh** button at the top of the layer list. By selecting the layers, you are adding them to the map. Add **Libraries** to your map.

To make sense of all the colors and symbols on the map, you will need to examine the legend. The legend is available from the View menu at the top of the page. Click on **Legend**. The legend will now appear on the left-side panel (Figure 3.8).

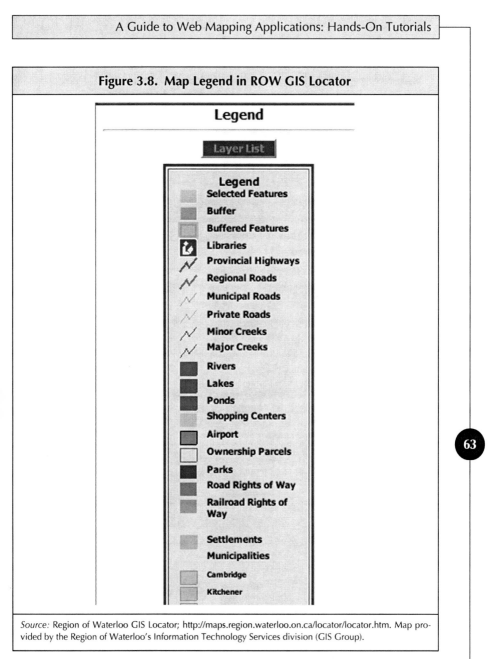

Figure 3.8. Map Legend in ROW GIS Locator

Source: Region of Waterloo GIS Locator; http://maps.region.waterloo.on.ca/locator/locator.htm. Map provided by the Region of Waterloo's Information Technology Services division (GIS Group).

The legend reveals the symbol given to represent libraries. Now it will be easier to find the libraries on the map. To learn more about the libraries, you'll have to active the library layer. Go back to the **Layer List**. You will notice that beside the Visible column, there is the Active column. The Active column allows users to activate one feature that they would like to investigate further. Activate **Libraries** and refresh the list.

Now you can utilize the map tools available to you at the bottom of the page. Click on the **Identify** button. Now click on one of the libraries. A table will pop up with address and telephone information about the library. Go back to the **Layer List** to select other layers, or unselect them if you wish to create a cleaner map.

Creating Custom Queries and Buffers

So far you have used queries to search for points of interest. If you go back to the Tools menu and click on **Query**, you will see that you can also perform queries on other categories such as Property by Address, Property by Roll Number, Street Name, and Services. However, you can also perform custom queries on any field in the Layer List. Custom queries can be performed from the Tools menu. Click on **Tools** and then click on **Create Custom Query**. Now you can search for specific schools, lakes, ice rinks, and so forth.

What you'll be doing next is locating a specific water body and then creating a distance radius buffer that will help you determine which parcels of land are hypothetically at most risk for flooding. To do this, you'll need to ensure that water and ownership parcels are visible in the Layer List. To return to the Layer List, click on **View** from the top toolbar.

Next, click on **Tools**, and then click on **Create Custom Query**. In the **Layer** dropdown select **Lakes**. In the **Field** dropdown select **Name**, and in the **Value** dropdown, select **Woolwich Reservoir** (Figure 3.9). Click on **Execute**.

Figure 3.9. Custom Query Search in ROW GIS Locator

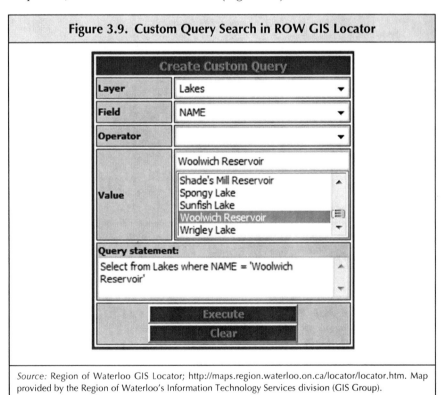

Source: Region of Waterloo GIS Locator; http://maps.region.waterloo.on.ca/locator/locator.htm. Map provided by the Region of Waterloo's Information Technology Services division (GIS Group).

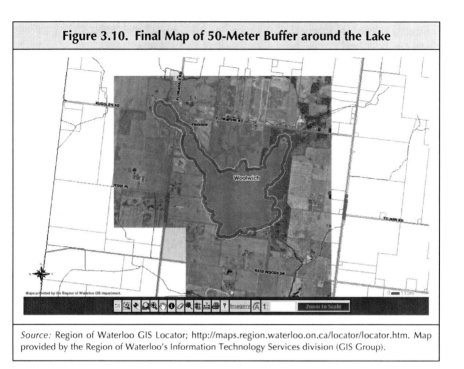

Figure 3.10. Final Map of 50-Meter Buffer around the Lake

Source: Region of Waterloo GIS Locator; http://maps.region.waterloo.on.ca/locator/locator.htm. Map provided by the Region of Waterloo's Information Technology Services division (GIS Group).

The map will now be zoomed into the Woolwich Reservoir. The left-side panel will display the attribute information for the lake.

Next you'll be creating a spatial buffer that will highlight the parcels of land that are as close as 50 meters to the reservoir and therefore may be considered at potential risk for flooding. To perform a buffer, you'll need to select the feature that you would like to create a buffer around. The bottom toolbar has a Select button. Click the **Select** button and then click on the Woolwich Reservoir on the map to select it. Now under the top Tools menu, select **Create Buffer**. Note that this feature is also available from the bottom toolbar. You will want to highlight features from **Ownership Parcels**, within a distance of **50 meters**. Click on **Create Buffer**. You now have all the property parcels selected that are within 50 meters to the lake.

To determine whether these properties have any buildings on them, turn on the aerial imagery. In the bottom toolbar, click on **Imagery**, and then select **2009 Ortho Imagery**. The map now has the aerial photograph in the background, with the other features on top (Figure 3.10). Now go back to the **Layer List** and activate the **Ownership Parcels**. Use the **Identify** tool (bottom toolbar) to learn more about the properties at potential risk.

Printing
The Print command is accessible from the bottom toolbar. Click on the **printer icon**. Add the title **Woolwich Reservoir**. Under **Map Notes**, add your name. Click on **Create Print Page**. A print page will be generated for you with your

title, name, legend, north arrow, and scale. These additional features are available to you automatically, making the creation of a cartographically correct map very simple. You may now print the map by going to **File** and **Print**.

Not all online mapping applications offer these types of cartographic elements, and yet there are others that offer even more advanced "final map" features. For example, some applications allow users to select the type of scale to insert, as well as offer air photo transparency levels and different text fonts and sizes. Some applications also offer several saving and sharing options, such as e-mail, URL addresses, and codes for embedding in personal webpages. The Region of Waterloo Locator doesn't encourage the sharing of its maps due to its strict licensing terms; however, not all municipalities are as limiting.

Editable Mapping Applications

This section provides readers with an overview of four excellent mapping applications that are commonly used for creating and sharing customized maps—Google Earth, Scribble Maps, Google Maps, and OpenStreetMap. All four applications support user editing, allowing features to be either imported into the program or edited on the map. Editable mapping applications expand the functionality that many other interactive applications offer by permitting users to mark up the maps and create their own thematic visual displays. These applications will prove to be powerful map making tools for library professionals wishing to create maps for visualizing information for presentations, events, and webpages and for creating digital projects. These applications are also being used by academics, students, and the general public, so library professionals may want to consider offering training workshops or online podcasts for these particular applications.

Although these editable mapping applications are user-friendly map making programs, they are also an extremely rich source of geographical and locational information. Programs like Google Earth are quite often used as a visual encyclopedia, where information can be looked up, zoomed in on, discovered, and analyzed. A program like OpenStreetMap is one of the richest sources of global information for topography, street details, and points of interest. These programs are valuable additions to the librarian's toolbox, especially for those offering reference or information services.

Google Earth

Google Earth is a free downloadable online application available for Windows, Mac, Linux kernel, FreeBSD, as well as for mobile viewers such as the iOS (Apple) and Android OS (*Wikipedia*, 2011). Since its release in 2005, Google Earth's imagery and geographic layers have been used by millions every year, driving society's interest in geospatial technologies and applications. Google Earth was one of the first online applications to make GIS technology entertaining, resourceful, and user friendly enough to be used by people of all ages, interests, and professions. Because of its global-wide popularity, Google Earth

66

is a popular tool used by educators and librarians alike to teach students about geography, mapping, and GIS.

Google Earth can be downloaded from http://www.google.com/earth/index .html. As of October 2011, the most recent version is Google Earth 6.1.

Google Earth: An Information Resource

With a collection of imagery and geographic layers larger than what most libraries can offer, Google Earth is a prime source for geographical and cultural information for librarians and academics. With world coverage satellite and air photo imagery, as well as its developing bank of street level photographs, Google Earth offers global awareness and geographic education. Image resolution varies between 15 cm and 15 m, with larger cities often being displayed using high-resolution aerial imagery. Figure 3.11 shows a high-resolution air photo captured in 2009 of the Staples Center in Los Angeles, California.

In the past few years, Google Earth has added historical aerial photographs and satellite images. A time slider tool allows the user to focus on a geographic area and then go back in time by sliding the years back. Some of the oldest air photos available in Google Earth go as far back as 1930. Figure 3.12 is a 1989 aerial image of the same area of Los Angeles, before the Staples Center was constructed.

Figure 3.11. High-Resolution Aerial Photograph of the Staples Center in Los Angeles, California, on November 14, 2009

67

Source: Google Earth; http://earth.google.com/.

Figure 3.12. Historical Aerial Photograph Taken on August 21, 1989, before the Staples Center Was Constructed

Source: Google Earth; http://earth.google.com/.

Chapter 2 discussed the many educational uses of Google Earth's imagery, so this will not be repeated; however, it may be beneficial to introduce some of the thematic layers that are available in this program. Many of these layers are considered to be helpful teaching aids by elementary and high school teachers.

Google Earth Layers

Google Earth has a large number of layers, accessible on the left side of the application, that allow users to overlay different types of information on top of the imagery. The layers are composed of points of interest, images, and details of many communities, with several being updated daily. Some of the layers are typically found on online maps, such as political borders and boundaries, streets, parks and recreation areas, weather, and business listings. Several other layers may be of interest to educators, students, librarians, and library users as well. Although there are too many to name them all, here are some examples of what is available:

- Buildings in 3D (users can also create their own 3D buildings and contribute them to Google Earth)
- Google Street View (360-degree panoramic views of streets of many cities in the United States, Canada, Mexico, Europe, Asia, Australia, and Africa)

- Oceans
  - Ocean Expeditions
  - Shipwrecks
  - Census of Marine Life
  - Animal Tracking
  - Marine Protected Areas
  - Ocean Sports
- Gallery (image-based resources)
  - 360 Cities—panoramic images of popular locations around the world (interior and exterior)
  - Earthquakes and Volcanoes
  - NASA
  - Rumsey Historical Maps
  - Location-based searches—Google Books, Google News, National Geographic, The New York Times, YouTube, webcams, Trimble Outdoor Trips
- Global Awareness (a collection of services spreading global awareness)
  - ARKive—endangered species
  - Earthwatch Expeditions
  - Unicef: Water and Sanitation
  - WWF Conservation Projects

To get a sense of how these layers work, let's explore a couple of them. You will be looking at photography, as well as the David Rumsey Historical Map Collection. If you haven't done so already, you will need to install the latest version of Google Earth at http://www.google.com/earth/download/ge/.

PHOTOGRAPHY

One of the richest sources of geographic and cultural information is photography, as it captures details that often cannot be expressed with words. Google Earth has an extraordinary collection of photographs, courtesy of both Panoramio and 360 Cities. Panoramio (http://www.panoramio.com/) is a popular Google-owned geolocation-oriented photo sharing website that allows the general public to upload their photographs and geotag their locations. There are millions of photos available across the globe, searchable and accessible from Panoramio's webpage as well as from Google Earth.

360 Cities (http://www.360cities.net/) is a commercial organization that offers customized high-resolution panoramic images of interior and exterior locations throughout the world. Its services are often used by the tourism industry. Its georeferenced, interactive photography collection is available on its website, as well as offered as a layer in Google Earth. Both 360 Cities panoramic imagery and Panoramio photography are available in Google Earth's Photos layer.

69

In the Layers panel, click on the **Photos** layer. To view the imagery, you will need to zoom into an area of interest. The Search panel is located at the top left corner. In the Fly To tab, type in **London, England** and press the **Search** key. You will be flown to London, England, and immediately you will notice a cluster of blue and red icons. The blue ones are images from Panoramio, and the red ones are panoramic images from 360 Cities. Using the navigation tools on the right side of the screen, zoom in further into London.

Explore some of the images available. To fly into a specific point of interest, simply type its name into the search field. Type in **Big Ben**. Manually zoom in a bit more until you're able to click on one of the red icons that represent 360 Cities imagery. Find an icon that's labeled **Big Ben** and click on it. A picture will pop up. Click on the picture to be taken into a panoramic view. You may notice that within the panoramic view there are other panoramic pictures also available. Some of these pictures lead to interior views.

360 Cities imagery is available for many areas of the world. Students and scholars studying geography, sociology, history, cultural studies, art, and the like may find these images very helpful. Other areas of the world with interesting imagery available include the following (remember, you can type in the city or point of interest into the Search panel):

- Easter Island, Chile
- Rome, Italy—St. Peter's Basilica
- Seiyun, Yemen
- Paris, France—Musée de l'Orangerie
- Toronto, Ontario—CN Tower

Millions of photos show the interiors of shops, markets, museums, art galleries, subways, historical buildings, and exterior photos show a range of themes, such as buildings, beaches, sunsets, transpiration, people, mountains, and deserts.

Another source of photograph imagery worth pointing out is available from the **Gallery** layer, under **National Geographic Magazine**, called the **Africa Megaflyover**. This product was sponsored by the National Geographic and created by biologist Mike Fay, who was interested in capturing photographs and videos of well-preserved land in Africa with the goal of promoting the importance of conservation and preservation. Fay flew over Africa in 2004, capturing images and sharing them with the world through the Africa Megaflyover layer (Rollins, 2010). Although these photos were taken from an airplane, they were taken at a low altitude, and thus are fairly high-resolution images. This resource allows users to zoom in further than is possible in all the other air photos available from Google Earth.

To view the high-resolution aerial photography, activate the Africa Megaflyover layer. The images available are denoted by a red airplane symbol. In the

Figure 3.13. Africa Megaflyover Layer Activated over Africa

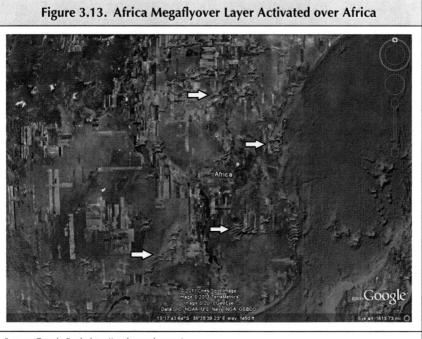

Source: Google Earth; http://earth.google.com/.

Search panel, type **Africa**, and click on the **Search** button. Zoom in until you see the red icons (Figure 3.13).

Double click on any of the red icons to fly into the area covered by the icon. Notice that a window pops up with additional information about the photo. To zoom further in to the photo, simply click on it and then use your navigation tools.

This layer provides the user with an excellent overview of the physical geography of Africa. Mike Fay's notes further offer his research and findings as they relate to the natural and cultural features of Africa, including flood plains, vegetation, forestry, farmland, salt marshes, villages, industries, and wildlife.

Finally, one cannot adequately describe the photography features in Google Earth without mentioning the popular Street View. Many areas of the world now have images available that were taken from the ground level. Images were captured by cameras installed on the roof tops of Google vehicles that were driven along major streets. Access to Street View imagery is available from the Navigation tools, symbolized by an orange person icon (Figure 3.14). Drag the icon onto the street of interest, and, if Street View is available for that particular area, you will be successfully dropped onto the street. With such high-resolution imagery, users can experience the surrounding culture—shops, cars, buildings, street signs, and so forth.

Figure 3.14. Google Earth's Navigation Tools with Street View Access

Source: Google Earth; http://earth.google.com/.

DAVID RUMSEY HISTORICAL MAP COLLECTION

As discussed in previous chapters, David Rumsey's collection of historical maps is freely available for viewing from the David Rumsey website at http://www .davidrumsey.com/. However, Google Earth also offers many of his georeferenced maps as a specific Rumsey Historical Maps layer. David Rumsey's collection includes maps representing the time between 1680 and 1930 in a variety of scales. The benefits of overlaying historical maps over current ones is that one can easily identify the locale of the map, as well as investigate any cultural changes that had occurred over time by referencing them to current features that one is familiar with (roads, railways, rivers).

To access Rumsey's historical maps, activate the layer by clicking on **Rumsey Historical Maps**, available from the **Gallery** layer. His maps are denoted by the compass icon. **Zoom** into your area of interest, and, if the icon is visible, then a map for that region is available. Click on the **compass** to learn about the map. Click on the **thumbnail image** to overlay the georeferenced map in Google Earth. If you like, you can add borders, labels, and roads on top of this map to help navigate it. These features are available from the Layers panel.

Simple Mapping

While most users enjoy Google Earth for its imagery and layers, there is in fact much more to the program. Google Earth's interface offers users features with a variety of mapping options. Users can add their own content—from basics like adding placemarks, drawing lines, and adding text to imagery, to dynamic contributions like adding photos, videos, links, and thematic map overlays—save it, and distribute it. The maps created can be shared via KML files, or they can be embedded into webpages.

This following section provide an overview of the features in Google Earth that can be used to create customized maps: adding placemarks, paths, text, and imagery, as well as working with external files. The user will soon see that although Google Earth is equipped with a large number of resources, the interface itself can be used as a mapping program.

THE BASICS

For this tutorial, you are going to create a vacation itinerary for Monterey, California.

1. In the Search box, type in **Monterey, California**, and press **Enter** or click on the **magnifying glass**.
2. To get a sense of what attractions are in Monterey, in the Layers panel, activate **Borders and Labels**, **Places**, and then **Roads.** Hover your mouse over the icons to see what places of interest are available.
3. You are interested in visiting the Monterey Bay Aquarium, so find that on the map. In the Search box, type in **Monterey Bay Aquarium**. You will see a number of results for the search, listed from A to J (Figure 3.15). You are interested in A, the aquarium on Cannery Road. To select one search result from the rest, right click on the **A** search result and then left click on **Save to My Places.**
4. Directly beneath the search result, there is a Places panel. This is where you manage all of your files. You will notice that the location of the aquarium has been saved to this panel. You can now clear your search results by clicking on the **X** at the bottom right corner of the Search panel.
5. Double click on the **Monterey Bay Aquarium** placemark in the **Places** panel. This will fly you to the location of the aquarium.
6. Now you're going to search for a restaurant where you can have lunch. Hover your mouse over the restaurants (**utensil icon**) to see what is available. Clicking on the icons will bring up a balloon with more information about the restaurant. Occasionally there will be URLs to a restaurant's webpage. Just west of the aquarium is a restaurant called Thai Bistro II. Locate that restaurant and add it to your Places. To do this, right click on the restaurant icon and then left click on **Save to My Places.**

73

Figure 3.15. Google Search Results for "Monterey Bay Aquarium"

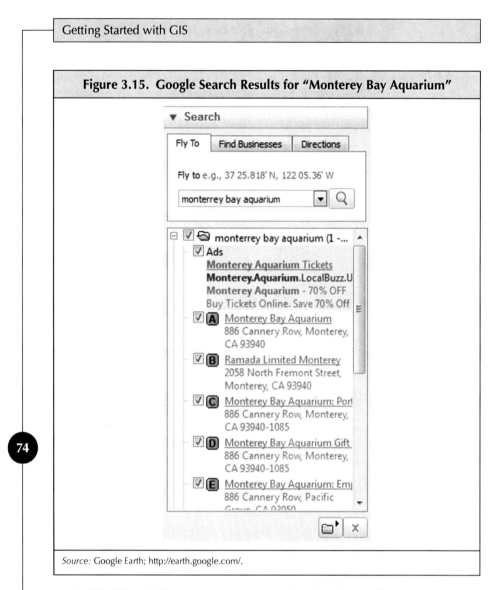

7. You'll be visiting one more attraction that day, but you're unsure what is available. Find the location of a tourist information bureau. In the Search box, type in "**tourist information.**" You will get a list of search results that are tourism related; however, the one you're interested in is the first one. Double click on this placemark, and then add it into your Places panel. Clear your searches.

8. From the **Layers** panel, remove **Places** (uncheck the box) so the map doesn't look overly cluttered.

9. Now you're going to find driving directions from the Aquarium to the restaurant and from the restaurant to the tourism bureau. In your Places panel, right click on the **Monterey Bay Aquarium**, and select **Directions from Here** (Figure 3.16).

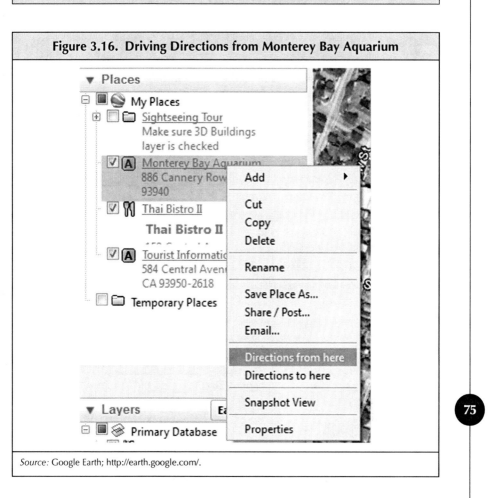

Figure 3.16. Driving Directions from Monterey Bay Aquarium

10. Right click on the **Thai Bistro II** placemark (in your **Places** panel) and select **Directions to Here**. The directions will be calculated and drawn on the map, as well as itemized as text in the Search panel. You will want to save these directions, so in the Search panel, right click on the direction command (it'll be the addresses of the two points) and **Save to My Places**.

11. Next you will query directions from the restaurant to the tourist information bureau. The steps are the same as outlined in steps 9 and 10. Complete this on your own.

12. You can click on the **Printable View** to get a Google Maps version of the map.

13. Now add one more feature to the map—a title. Click on the **placemark icon** (yellow pushpin) available from the menu at the top of the program.

14. Move the pushpin to the location where you would like your title to appear. In the window that popped up, type in your title. You can

change the pushpin icon by clicking on the pushpin symbol in the window. Once you have clicked on it, you will have a selection of icons to choose from, or, if you prefer, you can have no icon by clicking on the **No Icon** at the bottom of the symbology page. Click **OK** when you're done. You can further customize your title by altering the font size and color or the icon's size and color. This is done in the **Style, Color** folder in the same pop-up window. Click **OK** when you have finished customizing your title.

15. Your title information is available in your Places panel. If you need to alter your title, simply right click on it from the Places panel.

16. The contents of your Places can be neatly placed into a folder, which will allow you to save your map as a KML file and open it later or distribute it to others. To do this, in the **Places** panel, right click on **My Places, Add**, and **Folder.** Give your folder a name such as Vacation Day One. Then begin dragging all of the contents in the Places panel into the folder. If done correctly, when you minimize your folder, you shouldn't see anything else in the Places panel except for your folder and any default layers Google Earth added.

17. To save this map, right click on your new folder and then **Save Place As**, and save your map as either a KML or KMZ. Remember that a KMZ is a compressed version of KML. Either file format is fine.

18. Next time you are interested in viewing your map, simply double click on the KML file that you saved to your computer and it will automatically open Google Earth with your folder in it. You can also e-mail the KML file to others and they can open it in the same way.

If you are interested in adding additional information to your map, you can select from any of the features available from the top menu. You can add your own points of interest by using the placemark tool, you can draw lines with the paths tool, add polygons, measure distances, and more. Spend some time with some of the tools to see which ones may be of interest to you or to your library users.

Also take the time to explore the View menu, where you can switch between the Earth, Sky, Mars, and the Moon. You can also add cartographic elements to your map, such as a scale bar, a grid, and an overview map.

ADDING EXTERNAL FILES

Perhaps the most dynamic feature of Google Earth is enabling the importation of user content into the program, expanding its mapping capabilities considerably. The two most popular file imports are KMLs/KMZs and images. We'll take a look at KML and KMZ files first.

KML files can consist of images, graphs, text, points, lines, maps, and more. In the previous example you created a map and saved it as a KML file. If you upload this KML onto your webpage, others can download it and view it as well.

Similarly, you can download other people's or organization's KML files for use in Google Earth.

KML files have been popular for the past few years, but recently they have been gaining more acceptance as a GIS file alternative. Many websites that serve GIS data for download are also beginning to offer the same data in KML format for Google Earth use. Because many people don't have access to GIS programs, offering GIS information in a user-friendly format will increase its use and expand the user base. Examples of KML files from data resource websites include local information such as municipal park boundaries and playground locations, as well as global information like energy usage and climate data. Many organizations offer thematic maps in KML format. You may recall from Chapter 2 that the Ontario Geological Survey offers its geological maps in KML format.

KML files are also available from personal webpages as well as from Google Earth blogs, where people collect interesting findings they have spotted in Google Earth. In this case, the KML file is a simple placemark with coordinate information that will fly the user directly to the location of interest.

KML files can be easily downloaded and enjoyed by the end user. Creating KML files, however, is a bit more complex. KML file creation in Google Earth is very easy, as you saw for yourself. However, converting GIS files into KML files requires specific programs, which will be discussed in Chapter 4. To get a sense of how KML files can be opened in Google Earth, we're going to visit a few webpages that offer KML downloads.

The National Weather Service from the National Oceanic and Atmospheric Administration (NOAA) has a website dedicated to offering current weather-related information in KML/KMZ format. One can either visit the website and download the file of interest, or, alternatively, use Google Earth to browse the website and then automatically view the file.

To download files from an internet browser, visit NOAA's website, http://www.srh.noaa.gov/gis/kml/. You will see that there are a large number of weather-related themes available for Google Earth viewing. Under **Great Lakes**, click on **Water Temperature** and open the file. This file will now open in Google Earth (Figure 3.17).

To view the website within Google Earth, click on **Add** from the top menu. Then select **Network Link**. Paste, or type, in the URL into the Link box, and click on **OK**. The link becomes available in your Places panel. Double clicking on it will result in Google Earth opening a browser within the program. Under **Great Lakes**, click on **Wave Height**. Notice how the KML is automatically added into your Places panel and displays in the map view.

Another interesting collection of KML files is available from http://www.mgmaps.com/kml/, a page created by Christian Streng in 2009. This page offers a number of popular map overlays such as OpenStreetMap, Google Maps, Windows Maps, and Yahoo! Maps. If users find that Google Earth doesn't offer detailed enough

Figure 3.17. Water Temperature for the Great Lakes KML

Source: Google Earth; http://earth.google.com/.

street information, these KML files may help. Connect to his page, and beneath View in Google Earth, select the **OpenStreetMap** (Osmarender). Open this KML files and see how Google Earth transforms into OpenStreetMap. Zoom into the map to appreciate the detail. You may notice that even local roads are visible and labeled.

Some other websites worth mentioning include the USGS's earthquake webpage (http://earthquake.usgs.gov/learn/kml.php), which offers a collection of earthquake and geological data. A number of municipal websites offer a collection of municipal features in KML format, such as the City of Vancouver (http://data.vancouver.ca/datacatalogue/index.htm), City of Ottawa (http://www.ottawa.ca/online_services/opendata/info/index_en.html), City of Milwaukee (http://city.milwaukee.gov/DownloadMapData3497.htm), and Salford City (http://www.salford.gov.uk/opendata.htm).

One website worth highlighting is the City of Burlington, Vermont's KML Library (http://www.ci.burlington.vt.us/gis/download/). The KML Library includes a large collection of features such as city footprints, census block tracks, historical building footprints, bike paths, parks, real estate safety services, and zoning. Figure 3.18 shows parcel and zoning features displayed in Google Earth.

Figure 3.18. City of Burlington, Vermont, Parcels and Zoning KML files

Source: Google Earth; http://earth.google.com/.

One final website worth getting to know is Google Earth's Gallery, a collection of KML files compiled by the Google Earth community (http://www.google.com/gadgets/directory?synd=earth&preview=on&cat=all). KML files can be searched by keyword and categories include education, nature, ocean, travel, 3D buildings, and sports. The website is continuously updated with new files. On this website users can also receive free training on using Google Earth, from beginner to advanced tutorials. If you're interested in learning more about the features not discussed in this chapter, click on the **Learn** tab from the top menu.

The second type of external files that users can import is imagery. Images are supported in .jpg, .bmp, .tif, .tga, .png, .gif, .ppm, and .pgm formats. Images can be added from the **Add** menu along the top toolbar. Select **Photo**, and either add an image that is available from your computer or type in the URL of an online image. It's best to zoom into the area where you would like your photo to appear prior to adding it to the screen. Figure 3.19 shows several imported images.

Another way to add imagery into the program is to add it as an Image Overlay. An Image Overlay allows the user to drape the image precisely over Google Earth's satellite and air photo imagery. The image can be georeferenced with coordinate information so that its location corresponds to the Earth's location. The image can also be manually stretched, pulled, and aligned to fit exactly where the user would like it. Users who are interested in providing the public with

Figure 3.19. External Images Added to Google Earth

Source: Google Earth; http://earth.google.com/.

scanned images of collections, higher quality air photos, historical documents, maps, or photographs take advantage of this specific feature. Image Overlay is available from the Add menu.

This section has covered some of the more popular uses of Google Earth among library staff and their users. There are, however, many more features not discussed that you may want to learn about through online tutorials or by discovering on your own. The **companion website (http://www.neal-schuman.com/gis)** has additional tutorials, including georeferencing in Google Earth and creating KML files.

As mentioned, Google Earth is a free download, making it easy for people to use. With the popularity of KML files surfacing on websites, people are using GIS files that they previously could not. Google Earth has played an important role in assisting with geospatial information literacy, greatly contributing toward the increase of map usage and geographic awareness. To learn more about how organizations are using Google Earth, visit the Google Earth Outreach Showcase (http://earth.google.com/outreach/showcase.html).

Scribble Maps Pro

Scribble Maps Pro (http://pro.scribblemaps.com/) is an online mapping application that requires registration. Its counterpart, Scribble Maps (http://scribblemaps.com/), offers slightly less features and is available without registration. Scribble Maps Pro offers customizable map creations and supports the sharing of maps through various media. Its ease of use and accessibility make it a popular choice for the education sector as it does not require any downloads, and it offers a wide range of mapping features, such as map markups; measuring distances; importing KMLs, GIS files, and tables; and adding placemarks, text, shapes, and images. Scribble Maps Pro offers base maps from a number of sources such as OpenStreetMap, Google Maps, and Esri maps. Users will find this application similar to Google Maps, whereby one can search for a geographical area or a business. Completed maps can be shared with others through URLs, widgets for webpage embedment, and KML files. Out of the several mapping applications that are freely available to users, this one offers the most features and easy usability. Library staff looking to embed maps into their webpages will find this product to be the easiest to work with.

In the following tutorial, some of the more basic features of Scribble Maps Pro will be introduced. Although the product does offer the importation of external GIS files, the feature is somewhat limiting and often requires coordinate translations to work successfully. This feature will therefore not be covered in this tutorial.

Basic Mapping Features

Something unique to Scribble Maps Pro is its rich collection of drawing tools. Users have the ability to customize the colors of all drawn features—lines, polygons, irregular shapes, and markers. Included in the drawing menus are the following features:

- Pen tool for drawing straight or curved line segments
- Polygon pen tool for drawing polygons
- Scribble tool, a "free form pen" for doodling
- Line tool for drawing straight lines segments only
- Connected line tool for drawing connected lines
- Draw shape tool for drawing irregular shapes
- Draw rectangles
- Draw circles
- Place text
- Measurement tool (measures polygons, and lines)
- Markers (a variety of symbols available)
- Images—users can link images to their map (size is not adjustable)

The text is fully customizable as well, with a full range of fonts, colors, and sizes available. There are also a large number of placemark symbols to choose from. The base maps available include Google Maps (default), which includes satellite imagery, OpenStreetMap, CloudMade, CloudMadePlus, Astral, and Esri. Also available is a blank slate, with only a white background. Because of its customizability, Scribble Maps Pro is an excellent solution for those wishing to create maps of points of interest, "you are here" maps, and mashups.

81

Simple Mapping

In this tutorial, you will be creating a simple map of the three Library of Congress buildings in Washington, D.C. You will learn how to add placemarks, draw shapes, and add text and photos. To begin, log in to the Scribble Maps Pro page, http://pro.scribblemaps.com/. You will need to register or sign in.

1. From the bottom right corner, select **OpenStreetMap** as the base layer (Figure 3.20).
2. In the Search box, type in **Library of Congress, Washington**. Use the navigation tools on the right side of the screen to zoom in. You'll notice that the navigation tools are very similar to Google Earth's. Now you're going to highlight the **Thomas Jefferson Building** (1st Street SE, between Independence Avenue and East Capitol Street).
3. From the drawing menu at the top, select the **Draw Shapes** tool (Figure 3.21). Begin by clicking with your mouse on one of the corners of the building and draw around the perimeter of the building. When you have created a solid polygon, double click to finish drawing. You can change the color outline, fill, and opacity if you like (Figure 3.22).

Figure 3.20. Base Map Product Selection in Scribble Maps Pro

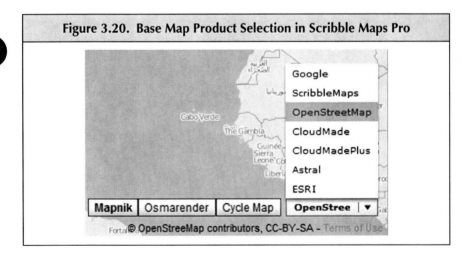

Figure 3.21. Draw Shapes Tool from the Scribble Maps Pro Menu

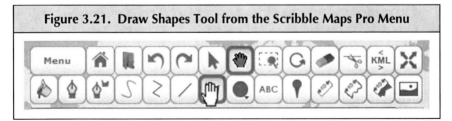

Figure 3.22. Drawing Shapes in Scribble Maps Pro

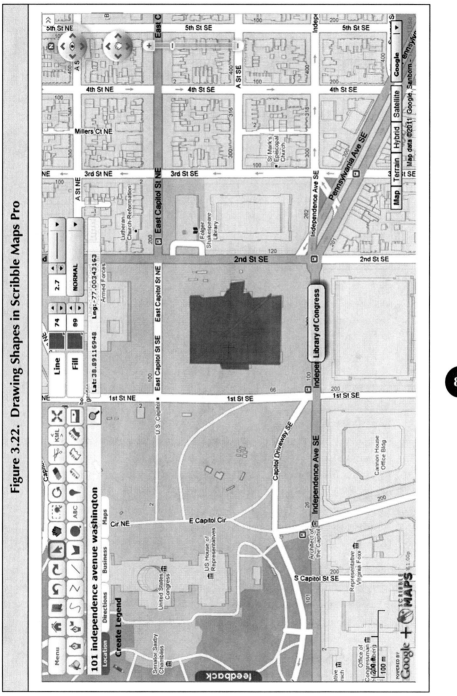

83

4. Next you will add text above the library building. Click on the **Place Text icon**, insert it above the building, and type **The Library of Congress—Thomas Jefferson Building**. Delete the default description text. If you need to edit the text, click on the **pencil** icon beside the text's layer in the frame on the right side of the page.

5. Now you are going to add an image of the Library of Congress building. Select **Add Image**, available from the top menu. The Library of Congress online image URL is available at http://www.loc.gov/visit/maps/floorplan.php?map=ljFront. Type this in the **URL/Link** location. Position the image where you would like it.

6. Next you're going to add three place markers, one for each of the Congress buildings. James Madison Memorial Library is located between 1st and 2nd Streets on Independence Avenue SE. The John Adams Building is located between Independence Avenue and East Capitol Street on 2nd Street SE. Click on the **Place Marker** tool from the top menu. Select a symbol of your choice. Position the symbol on top of one of the library buildings, and add a place marker title. Do this again for the other two libraries. Your map may look similar to Figure 3.23.

7. So far you have developed a fairly basic map, using place markers, text, drawing tools, and imagery. You're probably getting a good sense of these tools' potential. Next you are going to save the map as a KML file and view it in Google Earth. On the top toolbar, click on **Menu**, and select **Save KML**. Save the file to your computer.

8. Locate the file you had saved and double click on it to open it in Google Earth. You can now easily share this KML file with others.

9. From the **Menu**, you will also notice that you can save your map as an image, e-mail it, share it on Twitter and Facebook, and add it to your website using a widget. If you're going to add the map to your website, simply copy the widget code and paste it into your webpage's HTML code.

Although Scribble Maps Pro offers several features that are available in other mapping applications, it tends to be a bit more user friendly when it comes to creating KMLs, embedding maps into webpages, and adding photos to maps. Because it offers several different base map options, it provides users with views that are already familiar to them. One area that Scribble Maps Pro can improve in is its ability to work with imported KML files. Although it does have the feature to do so, the restrictions on it make it nearly impossible for novice users to work with it. The application that we'll look at next is Google Maps' My Maps. Although it doesn't offer as many features as Scribble Maps Pro, its KML importation feature is fabulous.

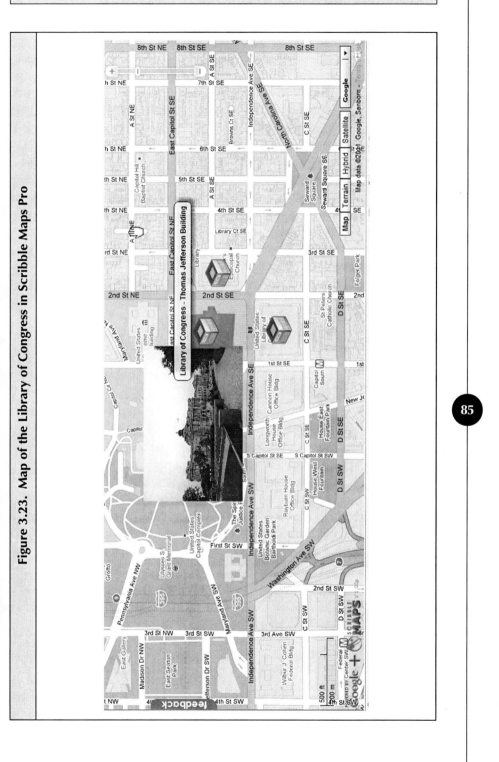

Figure 3.23. Map of the Library of Congress in Scribble Maps Pro

Google Maps: My Maps

Google Maps' My Maps is an online application that offers the creation of personalized maps. Its most popular tool is the placemark feature, utilized by millions of people to create map mashups or maps of points of interest. Additionally, Google Maps allows users to also mark their maps with lines and shapes, as well as text, photos, and videos. In many ways it is similar to some of the map making features that Google Earth offers; however, it is more conveniently accessible because it doesn't require a software download. Google Maps does, however, require free registration.

In this tutorial, you will be introduced to the map making features in Google Maps' My Maps application. Because this is a fairly straightforward program and without too many features, it is the most popular customizable map making application used by library staff and their patrons. The San Diego Library (http://www.sandiego.gov/public-library/locations/) is an example of a library that has created a map of its locations and embedded it into a webpage. In this tutorial, you will create a map similar to the one you created in Scribble Maps for the purposes of comparing the two products.

Getting Started

1. Go to the Google Maps webpage at http://maps.google.com/. Click on the top left **My Places** link (Figure 3.24). If you haven't logged in yet, do so now.
2. Directly below the **My Places** link is a link to **Create a New Map**. Click on that link.
3. Provide a title for your new map: **Library of Congress**. Add a description: **A Map of the Library of Congress and Surrounding Areas**. Make this map unlisted and click on **Done**.
4. Now you will edit the map and add personalized features to it. Click on the **Edit** button. You will need to zoom into the Library of Congress district. In the Search box type **Library of Congress, Washington**. Click on **Search Maps**, and zoom into the library buildings.

Figure 3.24. My Places Link Available from Google Maps

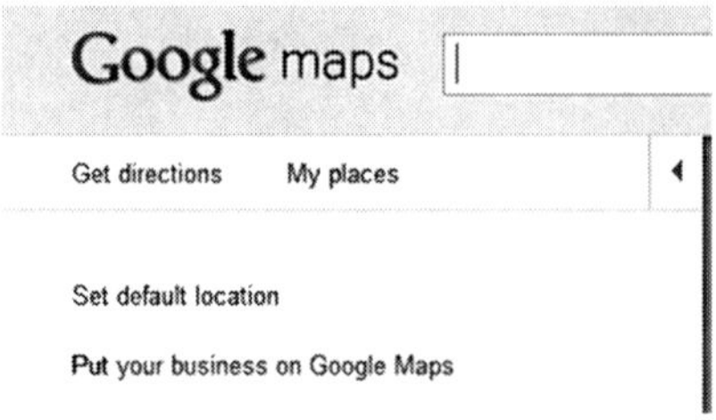

Source: Google Maps; http://maps.google.com/.

Figure 3.25. Edit Tools in My Maps

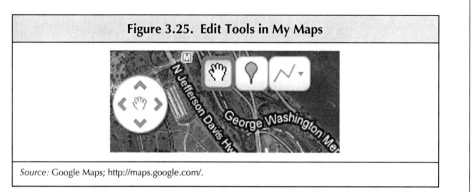

Source: Google Maps; http://maps.google.com/.

5. In your map view, there are three tools at the top of the map: edit, placemark, and drawing. Click on the **Placemark** tool and add a placemark for each library building with appropriate titles for each (Figure 3.25).

6. Now you're going to edit the Thomas Jefferson placemark. Double click on the Thomas Jefferson placemark that you created, and in the description box add a link to the Library of Congress Digital Collection: http://www.loc.gov/library/libarch-digital.html. Also, change the placemark icon to a question mark (click on the icon to open a selection of symbols). Note that you are able to import your own symbols as well.

7. Next you will highlight the Thomas Jefferson building by clicking on the **Draw** tool and follow the building outline with it. Select a color you wish, and leave the title blank. From this window, you can also insert an image. Click on the **Insert Image icon**. Type in the following URL image: http://blog.law.cornell.edu/files/2011/01/20050904-100-library-of-congress.jpg. When a user clicks on the building, the image will pop up.

Adding External Files

You're going to add some external resources to your map. You can import KML and KMZ files under 10 MB in size. This is an extremely valuable feature. Any application that supports KML imports is essentially providing users with a blank canvas to build an original masterpiece. With so many KML files available online, users can build customized maps to meet their personal needs.

To add KML files to our map, first download a few files onto your local computer. By downloading them first, you will know whether the size of the file falls under Google's 10 MB limitation. The District of Columbia has an excellent Data Catalog, available at http://data.dc.gov/. Visit this page, and scroll to

Figure 3.26. The District of Columbia Data Catalog

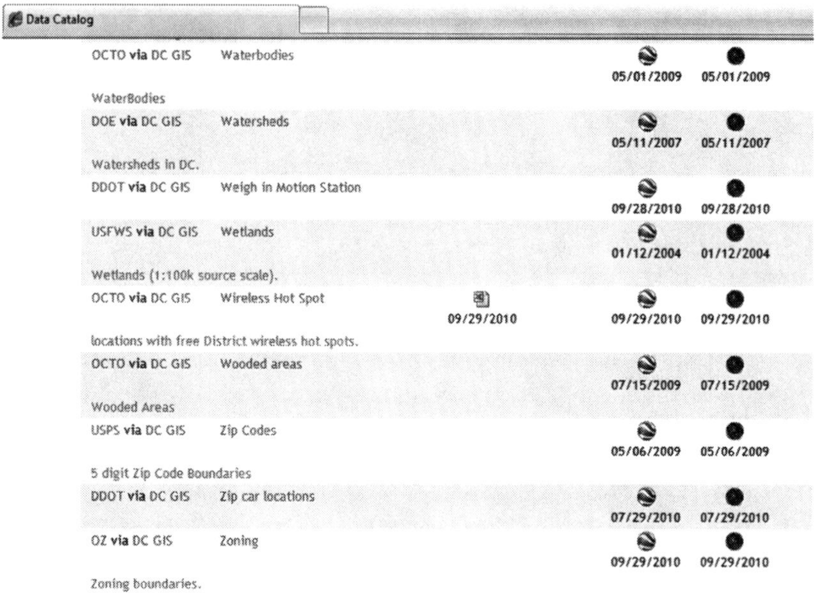
Data Catalog

OCTO **via** DC GIS	Waterbodies		05/01/2009	05/01/2009
WaterBodies				
DOE **via** DC GIS	Watersheds		05/11/2007	05/11/2007
Watersheds in DC.				
DDOT **via** DC GIS	Weigh in Motion Station		09/28/2010	09/28/2010
USFWS **via** DC GIS	Wetlands		01/12/2004	01/12/2004
Wetlands (1:100k source scale).				
OCTO **via** DC GIS	Wireless Hot Spot	09/29/2010	09/29/2010	09/29/2010
locations with free District wireless hot spots.				
OCTO **via** DC GIS	Wooded areas		07/15/2009	07/15/2009
Wooded Areas				
USPS **via** DC GIS	Zip Codes		05/06/2009	05/06/2009
5 digit Zip Code Boundaries				
DDOT **via** DC GIS	Zip car locations		07/29/2010	07/29/2010
OZ **via** DC GIS	Zoning		09/29/2010	09/29/2010
Zoning boundaries.				

Source: DC.gov; http://data.dc.gov/.

the bottom of the screen. You will see a list of features available in KML format (Figure 3.26)

You will download **Parks**, **Libraries**, and **Landmark Areas**. Locate each feature, and right click on its corresponding KML file (blue and white sphere). Select **Save Target As** and save the files to your computer.

1. Go back to your Google Map, and click on the **Import** link. In the **Import** window, browse to where you have saved your KML files. Import each one. You will have a combination of polygons and placemarks visible on your map. If you like, you can change the placemark icons to other symbols so you can differentiate between them.
2. When you have completed your map, click on **Done** on the left side of the page. Clicking on **Collaborate** will allow you to share your map with others.
3. Finally, you can print your map. The print menu is available from the top right menu of toolbars. Figure 3.27 shows the completed map in print mode.
4. You can also view your map in Google Earth. The link is available from the top right menu as well.

Figure 3.27. Map Created in My Maps

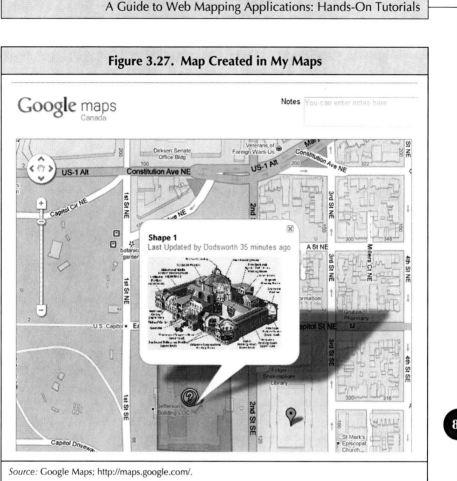

Source: Google Maps; http://maps.google.com/.

In this tutorial, you have learned how to draw shapes and how to add placemarks and KML files into Google Maps. If you take a look at the San Diego Public Library example mentioned earlier, you will see a large number of placemarks on the map. You certainly don't need to add every single placemark manually. Many users opt to import a KML file of placemarks. A list of addresses can be converted into KML files; this is covered in a separate tutorial in Chapter 5. To end this tutorial, you will learn how to embed Google Maps into a website.

Embed Maps into a Website

Google Maps can be embedded into webpages very easily. Once you have finalized all of your map details, zoom into your map to the level that you would like it to appear on your website. Directly above your map, you will see a menu of tools. The far right one is **Link**. Clicking on **Link** will provide you with the HTML code that you will need to copy and paste into your website's HTML code. You also have the option to customize the map. Clicking on the **Customize and Preview Embedded Map** will open a window with sizing options. From there, you can select the size of your map, change your zoom level if you need to, and then finally copy the HTML code. You will need to paste this code into your website's own source code.

You have just seen for yourself how easy it is to create a customized Google Map. You have also worked with Scribble Maps and are now able to compare the two products and decide on your own which product is better suited for your specific needs. Google Maps offers basic functionality, and sometimes simpler is better, especially for novice users who may feel overwhelmed with the many feature choices and mapping options.

One final mapping application you will learn to use is in this chapter is OpenStreetMap. You have already experienced using OpenStreetMap's map in the Scribble Maps Pro tutorial; however, what OpenStreetMap offers that no other mapping program does is the ability to permanently change the physical features represented in the map. This editing feature is what makes OpenStreetMap one of the most detailed sources for mapping information for the entire world.

OpenStreetMap

OpenStreetMap (http://www.openstreetmap.org/) is an editable map of the world created and updated by members of the user community. The detailed features available on the map have been created by interpreting aerial photography, paper maps, as well as users' personal knowledge and experiences of their local community. Many of the images and features can be downloaded and used for other projects. Because the project is a collaboration among individuals, groups, and organizations, nobody owns copyright to the product, thereby allowing everybody to use the data and maps as they wish.

OpenStreetMap is different from the other applications that we have examined in this chapter. The purpose of this application is not to create a personalized map, per se, but rather to contribute geographic and cultural details to the global database. A second purpose for this product is to act as a current detailed resource for street information. If library users are looking to find street maps of the world, you may want to point them to this resource.

In the following tutorial you will examine the features available in this product and compare them to Google Maps'. You will also learn how to contribute to this ongoing mapping project by permanently adding some of your own geographic knowledge of your communities to the map.

Getting Started

The general look and feel of the mapping program are similar to the others that you have already examined. You can search for geographic locations of places and points of interest and zoom into the areas of interest. You will begin by becoming comfortable with the interface.

Figure 3.28. Search Result for "Balepet, India" in OpenStreetMap

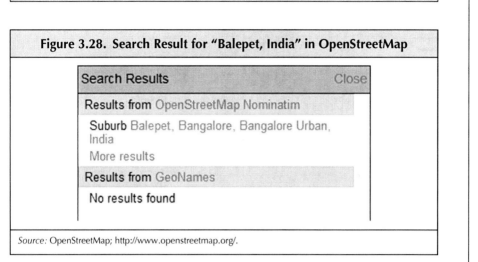

Source: OpenStreetMap; http://www.openstreetmap.org/.

Figure 3.29. Osmarender Layer in OpenStreetMap

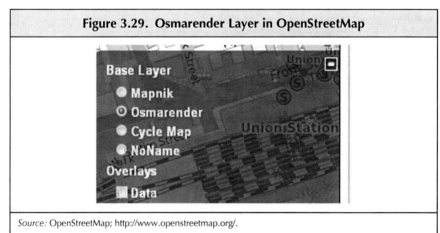

Source: OpenStreetMap; http://www.openstreetmap.org/.

91

Connect to OpenStreetMap (http://www.openstreetmap.org/). The search button is available on the bottom left of the screen, and the tools are available at the top of the screen. First, you'll zoom into Balepet, India.

1. In the Search field, type in **Balepet, India.** Select the result (Figure 3.28).
2. Use the zoom tool to zoom in even further. Notice the amount of street information available.
3. A number of base maps are shown that you can choose from as well. On the far right of the screen is an **X**. Click on that **X** to see the list of layers expand. Select each layer to see how it differs from the others (Figure 3.29). For this tutorial, click on **Osmarender.**
4. Now compare this street map with one you will create in Google Maps. In Google Maps, search for **Balepet, India**, and zoom in accordingly.

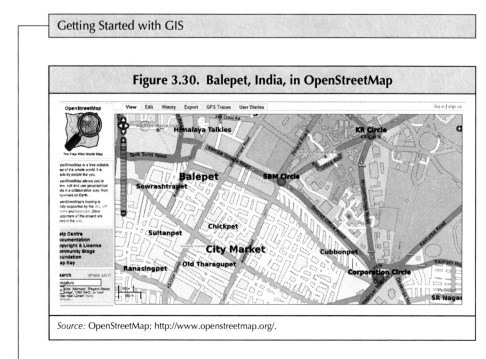

Figure 3.30. Balepet, India, in OpenStreetMap

Source: OpenStreetMap; http://www.openstreetmap.org/.

Switch your view from imagery to **Map** (along the top of the page) to compare the map information between the two products.

5. You will notice that OpenStreetMap has more topographic detail as well as additional local roads. Figures 3.30 and 3.31 show the two maps.

Adding and Editing Features

OpenStreetMap allows users to add and edit features on the map. Buildings can be added, streets can be altered, bends of rivers can be adjusted, and more. The changes made using the application can either be made on the users' account by saving the changes (they sign in, and only they can see the changes) or published, with changes made permanently, and instantly, on the global database for everybody to access. For this tutorial, you will be saving changes without publishing them so that you don't unintentionally edit correctly mapped information.

1. To begin, you will need to log into your account. If you haven't done so already, you will need to register and log in. If you are registering, e-mail confirmations may take several minutes. The log-in link is on the top far right corner of the page.

2. Once you are logged in, zoom into **New York City**. Zoom in further to any area of the city that you would like. Find an area that has buildings and streets. You are going to edit the visible features by clicking on the editing tool available from the top menu. Click on the **Edit** tool.

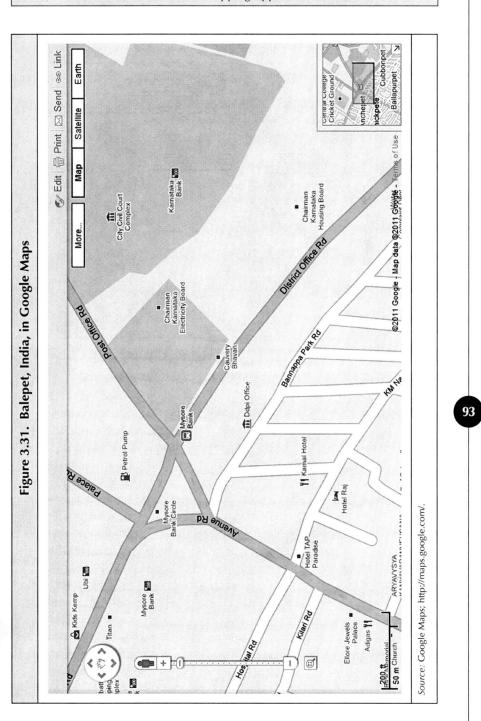

Figure 3.31. Balepet, India, in Google Maps

93

Figure 3.32. Edit Tool in OpenStreetMap

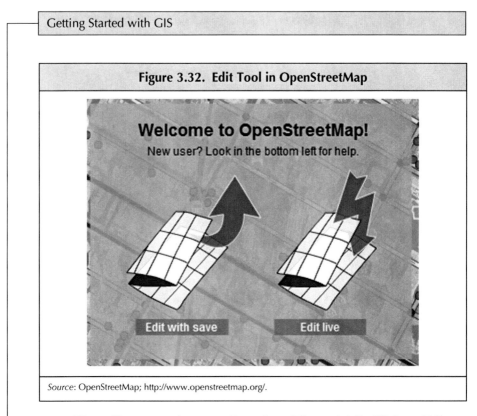

Source: OpenStreetMap; http://www.openstreetmap.org/.

3. You will now see the two edit options (Figure 3.32). Click on **Edit with Save**.

4. Now, all points and lines are editable. Feel free to move around any features you see by clicking and dragging them with your mouse.

This editing feature is particularly useful for constructing maps with high precision. Users who are very knowledgeable about local geographic and cultural features can adjust their representations on the map to accurately position them. Users may be familiar searching Google Maps for features and realizing that the locations are not always accurate. OpenStreetMap provides the benefit of simply dragging the feature from its approximate location to its precise one.

5. You will also notice a list of features at the bottom of the screen that you can add to the map. Practice by dragging some of the features onto the map. Click on a point of interest and drag it onto the map. After each feature you drop, you will need to click on the **Save** button (bottom right corner) in order to add the next feature. To delete the feature, you can click on the **Esc** button on your keyboard while your feature is selected on the map.

When users find details missing on the map, they can add from a large collection of point or line features. Some of the features include eateries, hotels, hospitals, bus stops, pharmacies, police stations, parking lots, and supermarkets. Each feature also has a dropdown menu with additional subfeatures. You can add names to the features as well.

6. To add lines to the map, simply click on the map and draw your route. To edit any of the street information, click on the street and your street attributes will be made available to you at the bottom of the screen.

Upon completion of editing the map, you can save a copy of it. Click the **Export** tool along the main menu, and you will get a choice of map backgrounds and image formats. Your page view will save as an image; however, you will notice that advanced features such as accompanying titles and legends are not available. This is because OpenStreetMap is not a map making program but rather an interface for collecting and distributing data. Because of the number of contributions made already to this application, many trust it as a resource for highly detailed street and topographic data. This application was introduced to users in this chapter as a map resource, but expert users will certainly find many more uses for it.

OpenStreetMap data are compatible with many other programs and therefore can be used for advanced purposes. Expert users can export OpenStreetMap data and convert into other program files for use in advanced GIS applications as well as for Google Earth usage. Data distribution is one of the main uses of OpenStreetMap among GIS users, developers, and programmers.

Conclusion

The tutorials in this chapter introduced the reader to a number of popular online mapping applications that are regularly used by educators, scholars, and professionals for geographic information and mapping purposes. Working knowledge of government mapping projects, along with popular mapping applications, provides users with the tools necessary to share this resource knowledge with others, embed the technology into their work environment, and spark an interest to delve deeper into the endless possibilities of incorporating GIS technology into library services. Chapters 5 and 6 will provide examples of case studies and tutorials for using GIS technology specifically for library-related services and projects.

The skills gained so far provide readers with a thorough understanding of what is possible and what can be done with online mapping applications. The reader has gained geographic awareness and spatial literacy skills and now is ready to move forward to learning about more advanced uses of GIS technology. Chapter 4 introduces the reader to geospatial data, GIS software, and GIS-related tools that will expand map making possibilities even further.

References

Rollins, Jared. 2010. "National Geographic: Africa Megaflyover." *Teaching and Learning with Google Earth Blog*. April 26. http://sites.duke.edu/tlge/2010/04/26/national-geographic-africa-megaflyover/.

Wikipedia, 2011. "Google Earth." *Wikipedia*. Last modified February 1. http://en.wikipedia.org/wiki/Google_Earth.

Chapter 4

An Introduction to GIS Data and Software

Introduction: GIS Data and Software

Even though there are many online mapping resources available for mapping projects, they can be somewhat limiting for users needing to work with specific features or data layers. As noted in previous chapters, using GIS can be as simple as connecting to a map server and creating a map with the data packaged within the product. Unfortunately, not all data features are made available in online mapping programs. Users looking for less common features, such as locations of water wells, for example, will not likely find that GIS data layer in an online mapping program. Therefore, there are some disadvantages to these types of products because the user is limited to using the features that are packaged into the product. One workaround, however, is to work with a GIS program that permits users to import external data. This will of course create endless mapping opportunities, as any feature can be added into the program, including something as localized as water wells or even telephone poles. For these types of customized mapping capabilities, users turn to GIS software programs. Unlike interactive online mapping programs, GIS software, typically available for desktop use, offers a broad range of GIS features, with mapping being only a part of it.

GIS software applications can be utilized not only to create professional looking maps but also to assist with digitization projects, file conversions, and geocoding. Because of the multidisciplinary and academic nature of mapping, there is no doubt that some library users will be inquiring about its use and access to it. Hence, it is crucial that the library staff become acquainted with GIS software programs' capabilities in order to deliver successful reference and subject liaison services.

Alongside having working knowledge of a GIS program, users must also understand the fundamental principles of the GIS data that get imported, or added, into the program. A GIS program on its own is useless without the data. The data, often collected as individual features of interest, is the most important element of map making. This chapter will introduce you to GIS

97

data, GIS software programs, and their accessibility in libraries. Chapters 5 and 6 will specifically discuss the use of GIS programs in library digitization projects, in library administration, as well as in library services.

GIS in Libraries

GIS services are offered at many public, academic, and special libraries. The extent of GIS services offered in libraries differs tremendously from one library to the next, however, with some having a dedicated GIS department and others consisting of only one or two specially trained staff members. Although traditionally GIS services have been a segregated service offered by specially trained staff members, the increased use of GIS in libraries makes it unrealistic and inefficient to continue offering GIS services by only a limited number of staff. Because GIS software, data, and training have become more widely accessible, many elements of a GIS service can be offered by all liaison librarians and reference staff.

One of the most popular uses of GIS software among library users is to create a customized map. There are two essential components of map creation—software and data. For libraries that have an established service already, GIS software is often available on public library computers. Library professionals can be trained on teaching library users the basics of getting started with the software; however, it is recommended that a GIS specialist still be made available to answer any technical or geographic questions the users may have. Providing users with additional training resources such as self-paced guides and tutorials will allow them to gain their own GIS skills. Alternatively, a number of GIS software programs can be installed on personal computers, so, if the library doesn't offer public access to GIS software, the librarian can recommend a number of free or licensed GIS products.

Besides accessing software, library users are often interested in accessing data. Many libraries have their own collection of GIS data, often collected and managed by the library's GIS or map librarian. Library staff should become acquainted with the data available in order to point the users in the right direction. Again, if more advanced assistance is required or if the new user requires training, then a GIS specialist should be made available to them. Additionally, there are fabulous GIS data resources available online as well.

This chapter will provide you with the geospatial literacy skills needed to comfortably and confidently meet the basic GIS needs of users. Reference staff should never feel that GIS software and data are dauntingly difficult requests that should be automatically forwarded to GIS librarians. Too many times, library staff take the "it's not my field/not my problem" approach and shut down the patron's request before fully listening to what the user needs. Perhaps it's just an online map, or information about training resources, but whatever is being asked, it should be understood by the librarian. Once the tutorials in this chapter are completed, all future GIS-related questions asked by library users should be understood enough by the librarian to know whether they are simple requests or complex ones that do in fact require a GIS specialist's assistance.

GIS Data

So far in this book, you have been exposed to map creation using online resources without needing to import any data. The data were already available to use in the mapping application, and users simply selected the features that they wanted displayed. One of the limitations of online mapping programs is that most of them don't support the importation of external files. This is precisely why many users choose GIS programs.

You may recall that some of the interactive websites also offered data for download. Users can search for the government agency of interest to access the files. Geoportals are another common resource for provincial/state or national level data. Many libraries also compile data resources of interest to their users and list them on their websites. Academic libraries in particular have well maintained lists of available data resources.

Working with websites that offer data for download is quite a bit different than working with those that offer online mapping. There are a few fundamental data concepts that need to be understood first before any data can be searched and downloaded. Because portals offer data in different formats, and in different projections, one will need to know a bit about the data options available in order to select the most appropriate data.

99

Data Types

Geospatial, or GIS, data are an ensemble of files that tells the software program how and where to display the information graphically. Two data models are used widely in mapping data: vector and raster.

Vector Format

Geospatial data in vector format describes features of the earth as points, lines, and polygons. For example, locations, such as addresses of customers, can be represented by points, streams and roads can be represented by lines, and parcel or administrative boundaries can be represented by polygons. Users can load one, two, or all three vector types into a GIS program. Each vector file is still separate and can be turned on and off individually. Those who have used the interactive mapping programs have already been exposed to vector files. Users wanting to create a map of neighborhood parks, for example, may activate the park boundary file, the roads line file, and the city name point file.

These vector files come in a special format. Just like .txt is read by Word and .dbf is ready by Excel, GIS programs read a special file type called the shapefile (.shp). So to create a map of parks, as mentioned, one would need to get a hold of three shapefiles: parks, roads, and cities. All GIS software programs read shapefiles, and almost all GIS files are made available in this format. The shapefile displays information that it reads from the attribute table (.dbf). The shapefile is a collection of files, one of which is the attribute table—the descriptive data that GIS links to map features. A GIS program can read other GIS files as well. Although shapefile is the most popular type of GIS file, many GIS programs also support text files, AutoCAD files, and a list of other less commonly used file formats.

Raster Data

The second data model is the raster data set. Raster files are image formats, such as .jpg and .tif, that have been georeferenced to display properly in a GIS program. The raster model uses a grid or cell as a unit to store data, with each cell populated with coordinate information. Air photos and satellite imagery are both examples of raster files. Raster formats can also include nonphotographic files such as an image of rivers, or buildings, or a scanned image of a map. Image data offers a quick way to access spatial data for a large area and is more cost and time effective than trying to collect layers of data like streets, rivers, and buildings one at a time. However, unlike vector data, one can't turn off any features in an image. An image such as an air photo is often used as either a base map or a point of reference in maps.

A raster data set is often composed of one or two files. Most GIS programs support a large variety of raster formats: .tif, .jpg, MrSID (.sid), and grids, are the most commonly used image formats. The tiff image either has accompanying world files (a world file is a text file with coordinate information) or stands alone as a GeoTIFF. A GeoTIFF has coordinate information in the header of the image and can be read only spatially by a GIS program. Other graphic programs will also read the GeoTIFF, but they will ignore the header and will simply display the image as a regular tiff image format. MrSID is another popular image format—it is a compressed image file and very popular with orthoimagery (air photo) industries as it compresses images by up to 20 times. So instead of offering users an image of a city 20 GB in size in tiff format, it will be compressed into a 1 GB MrSID format image. MrSID, however, is a proprietary image format, and not all GIS programs support it.

Some of the most popular raster files in libraries are digitized air photos, or orthoimagery. Air photos have been taken at a specific point in time, at specific locations, and they capture tremendous amounts of information about natural and human-made features. There is very little inaccuracy with air photos, because they are captured by cameras. Vector data sets, on the other hand, have been created by humans who interpret the features on the earth and create graphics based on them.

Data Projections and Coordinate Systems

Because of the large number of projection types available, many data resources offer data in a number of different projections. It is therefore important to understand the concept of projections and coordinate systems so that you select the most appropriate one for your GIS project. This section will provide a basic introduction to map projections and coordinate systems. The **companion website (http://www.neal-schuman.com/gis)** provides a list of resources that explain the concepts and theories in much more detail.

Most people who have used a map are familiar with the concept of geographic coordinates. The geographic coordinate system is a reference system that uses latitude and longitude to define locations on the surface of the Earth. Geographic coordinates can be expressed as degrees/minutes/seconds (DMS), such as 92° 30' 00" W, or as decimal degrees (DD), such as −92.5. The survey model used to match the location of features on the ground to coordinates and locations on a map is the datum (the initial point of reference). In North America, early topographic maps were based on the North American Datum 1927 (NAD27). There are still data available in this datum. More recent data are based on a North American Datum 1983 (NAD83). The Global Positioning System uses an Earth-centered datum called the World Geodetic System 1984 (WGS84). When searching for data, you will likely come across one of these three datum systems. They are commonly referred to as NAD27, NAD83, or WGS84.

The coordinate system specifies the units used to locate features in two-dimensional space. A "geographic" coordinate system reads and displays the map as latitude and longitude; however, it does not take into account the differences between the sphere of the earth and the flat map. There will therefore always be some degree of distortion on the map. Distance and area, for example, will not be completely accurate. Because of this, the geographic coordinate system is generally used only for locating positions on the Earth's surface.

Because map accuracy is critical for so many applications, projected coordinate systems are used to minimize some degree of the distortion. All map projections distort the shapes of the features being displayed to some degree, as well as the measurements of area, distance, and direction. The distortions are usually very minimal when working with a relatively small geographic area such as at the city level. When mapping areas at the national or global level, the distortions become much more obvious. For example, you may recall seeing a world map that distorts certain countries, such as Greenland, making it appear much larger than it really is.

The resources available from the **companion website (http://www.neal-schuman.com/gis)** describe a large number of different projection types. Basically, there are different projections for different geographies, as well as for different features that are to remain undistorted (shape, size, distance, etc.). When working with North American data, a common projected coordinate system is the Universal Transverse Mercator (UTM). The Mercator is a conformal projection, preserving angles and approximates shapes, but it distorts distance and area. However, when working with smaller geographies, this distortion is not

101

overly noticeable. The UTM system divides the Earth into 60 longitude zones, numbered 1 through 60, with zone numbering increasing in an easterly direction. When data are created for a specific zone, the distortion is reduced even further.

Projected coordinate systems such as the UTM do not use latitude and longitude as measurements of reference. They use "eastings" and "northings," which are measured in meters. For example, the geographic position 43° 38' 33.24" N, 79° 23' 13.7" W is translated to 630084m east, 4833438m north using the projected system. When GIS data are available in the projected UTM system, it will be commonly noted as UTM and the zone number. Because the datum needs to be known as well, all GIS files will be described with their coordinate system and datum, such as UTM, Zone 7, NAD83.

Luckily, novice GIS users don't need to worry too much about which zone their area of interest is in or which ideal projection to use. GIS data for specific geographic areas are usually available to users in one or two different projection types, and really either one will work. They may not always be available in UTM, however. The State Plane is another popular one, used in the United States for state level data. With today's user-friendly GIS programs, the applications will accept all projections and will automatically make sure all files work well together. For precise mapping, however, users may wish to convert one projection to another, which is also a feature available in many GIS programs.

Once the user has developed a basic understanding of projections and coordinate systems, he or she is ready to begin the journey of searching, filtering, and selecting data from the mass collection of geospatial resources available. Data selection is one of the most important elements of map creation, because, although the data may be widely available and easily accessible, not all data are the same, often varying in quality and accuracy.

GIS Data Selection

As you search for GIS data either for yourself or for your library users, you will go through a process of making a wish list and investigating data that meet your criteria. Recall that in order to create a map you will need individual data files (i.e., shapefiles) for each feature you would like displayed. When searching for data to use in your map, keep in mind that your output, your map, or data analysis, is a reflection of your data input. With so many geospatial resources available, you can afford to be selective based on your feature standards. Geospatial data are available from both reputable and nonreputable sources. Libraries collect and acquire geospatial data from both governmental and commercial organizations. Libraries will also promote, download, and use data that are available from the Internet, as data are available and accessible from the web just as easily as text information is. Analyzing your data sets and knowing which one to use, however, is critical when working with unknown sources. A number of factors will influence which data resource to point your library users to: geographic area of interest, data features, currency, and licenses. Depending on these factors, you will need to narrow down the data resources available to the user.

Geographic Extent

The geographic area of interest is the most important factor in determining which resource to consider for meeting data needs. Is data required for a specific neighborhood or for a foreign country? Libraries generally have an excellent collection of data for their own local county, and numerous online resources offer national data for Canada, the United States, and the world. Data for specific countries outside of North America can often be more difficult to locate and access and may require special purchasing. Once the geographic extent is known, the unlimited amount of data available can be narrowed down considerably.

Geographic Features

Which features (often referred to as "layers") is the library user interested in? Some features are harder to find than others, and some features are basic enough that they can be accessed from several data providers. You will need to locate a data provider that offers the specific features of interest and preferably one that includes rich attribute information and metadata. A feature or layer is not very useful when the attribute information associated with it is incomplete or nonexistent. Take street files, for example. Most data vendors and government organizations offer basic topographic information such as street networks. Not all street layers are the same, however—some may consist of only highways, and others may include details such as local roads and bike trails. The attribute tables will certainly differ as well. One organization may provide you with a simple line file and a much stripped down database of information, and yet another one may provide you with a street file that includes names of streets, traffic direction, speed limits, and travel time.

Data that are accompanied with metadata will provide the user with a description of the data. Metadata will often include a list of the attributes available, the data set's currency, survey methods, coordinate information, geographical extent, and more. Reading the metadata beforehand will prevent the users from downloading a data set that doesn't meet their criteria.

Currency

GIS is still considered a relatively new field, and therefore historical data sets are not easily obtainable. Unlike with maps, users will have a tough time accessing street and building data from the turn of the twentieth century. Data sets are usually current, although there are many data sets that have not been updated for ten years or so and prove to be less useful. Users who are interested in designing a site plan for a new restaurant, for example, may want to research all the buildings around the site. Using data that are 10 years old can be obviously quite damaging.

Data users therefore need to consider the data's currency when making resource selections.

Licensed Data

Depending on the organization, agency, and age of the data, the use of the data may be under certain licensing terms. Users should be aware of the terms in order to understand the limitations. Essentially, all data are free of licensing restrictions when used for educational, nonprofit purposes. Users should read the license agreements carefully when hoping to print or publish maps created with the data sets.

Data Access

One of the most challenging aspects of a GIS service is identifying users' needs, acquiring resources to meet those needs, and managing and maintaining the resource collection. Although today many libraries have already developed a geospatial service, some still have yet to build a collection from ground zero.

A GIS collection is comprised of both governmental and commercial sources. Organizations offer options and products that present the user with different levels of access to digital geospatial information. Much of the data that are available publicly today are government data at the federal and provincial/state levels. The ease of download and interoperability of many government data files has led do the widespread integration of similar data files across different GIS coverages. Most data sets are made available in the Esri shapefile format, enabling compatibility with different GIS software programs. GIS data sets are generally accompanied by detailed metadata that assists in the selection, cataloging, and description of the collection.

Data that are purchased from an organization that specializes in data creation, manipulation, and distribution is usually accompanied by value-added information. Commercial companies simply take data that have been already digitized—such as national and provincial parks or major and minor waters—and they repackage it into a product that offers more than what governmental resources would offer. Most of the value is in the attribute table and/or in the quantity of data available. Commercial data are often provided with free yearly updates and excellent metadata files.

Some of the most widely used data are those freely available from online portals or resource websites. Library users often find online data more easily accessible because they can access it at their convenience. There are many reputable online sources for data. Many are government initiatives, offered by different levels of government, but some very excellent national geoportals also offer a one-stop shop for data and maps. A list of data resources is available on the **companion website (http://www.neal-schuman.com/gis)**. Geoportals have become very popular with Map and GIS librarians because they provide an organized way to store and share data. Data can be easily updated, and users can receive notice when new or updated data arrive. By having data accessible online, libraries don't need to manage the data on their own server. And because many libraries often collect the same data, portals eliminate duplicate storage and maintenance of the data.

National Geospatial Data Resources

Canadian

- GeoBase
  http://www.geobase.ca/
- GeoConnections Discover Portal
  http://geodiscover.cgdi.ca/web/guest/home
- Geogratis, Natural Resources Canada
  http://geogratis.cgdi.gc.ca/geogratis/en/index.html

American

- American FactFinder, U.S. Census Bureau
  http://factfinder.census.gov/servlet/DatasetMainPageServlet
- Cumulus Portal for Geospatial Data, USGS
  http://cumulus.cr.usgs.gov/
- Geospatial One Stop
  http://www.geodata.gov/
- National Atlas of the United States
  http://www.nationalatlas.gov/

Many more resources are listed on the **companion website (http://www.neal-schuman.com/gis)**.

105

Examples of Online GIS Data Resources

This section will use examples of online data resources to demonstrate how to effectively search for and download GIS data. Although there are thousands of geospatial portals and projects available, seeing examples of a couple of them will provide enough familiarity to the readers to be able to successfully navigate around all online data resources. The two data products that will be examined are the City of Toronto's Toronto.ca/open and the Geospatial One Stop (GOS) American geoportal.

Toronto.ca/open

The City of Toronto's Toronto.ca/open project is an example of data liberalization in Canada. Data that used to be under strict licensing terms, and difficult to access, are now freely available to the general public to do what they wish to with the data. Releasing information about the city benefits everybody, and the philosophy of opening data access to municipal information has been adopted by a number of Canadian cities, including Edmonton, Ottawa, and Vancouver. Hopefully this model will eventually be used by all cities in Canada.

The City of Toronto's Open Data webpage is available from http://www.toronto.ca/open/index.htm. On the main page is a link to the data catalog from the Get the Data button. Clicking on this button will open the catalog, consisting of 35 or so GIS data files. The types of GIS files available include these:

- Municipal Address Points
- Bikeways
- Business Improvement Areas
- Licensed Child Care Centres
- Election Results
- Festivals and Events
- Forestry Land Cover
- Parks

Figure 4.1 shows the data catalog, with three columns—the feature description, the GIS file format, and the currency. If you take a look at the GIS file formats available, you will see that many files are available in the Esri shapefile format. This is the file format that will be downloaded for use in a GIS program.

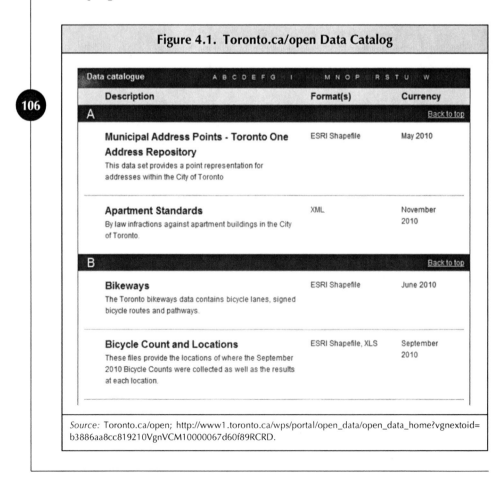

Figure 4.1. Toronto.ca/open Data Catalog

Source: Toronto.ca/open; http://www1.toronto.ca/wps/portal/open_data/open_data_home?vgnextoid=b3886aa8cc819210VgnVCM10000067d60f89RCRD.

Figure 4.2. Parks Metadata Information

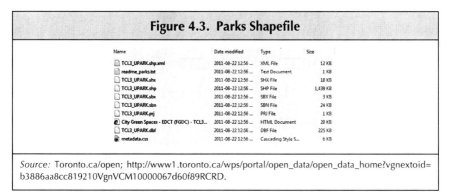

Data Catalogue » Parks	
Owner	Parks, Forestry and Recreation
Currency	May 2010
Format	ESRI Shapefile, WGS84
Projection	MTM 3 Degree Zone 10, NAD27
Attributes	The parks data set provides the boundaries and park names for over 2000 public green areas within the City of Toronto. Each park is described with a unique identifier, name and feature code.
Contact	Geospatial Competency Centre gcc@toronto.ca
Data	
	• May 2010 (MTM 3 Degree Zone 10, NAD27) • May 2010 (WGS84 - Latitude / Longitude)

Source: Toronto.ca/open; http://www1.toronto.ca/wps/portal/open_data/open_data_home?vgnextoid=b388 6aa8cc819210VgnVCM10000067d60f89RCRD.

This tutorial will involve working with the Parks shapefile. Clicking on the Parks description link will open the file's metadata page (Figure 4.2), providing information on the data's owner and the file's projection information and description. The file's projection is available in both Modified Transverse Mercator (MTM) and the World Geodetic System (WGS), using the North American Datum 1927 (NAD27).

To download the shapefile, click on one of the projection files beneath Data. This is a zipped file and will need to be unzipped. Shapefiles are commonly zipped because they consist of several files. Click on the file and save it to your computer. Then locate the file on your computer, unzip the folder, and take a look at the files. Figure 4.3 shows the Parks shapefile unzipped.

All the files that are associated with the Parks shapefile are named the same, with only the extensions differing. Remember that all files accompanying the shapefile (.shp) are required to display the data in a GIS program. When the

107

Figure 4.3. Parks Shapefile

Name	Date modified	Type	Size
TCL3_UPARK.shp.xml	2011-08-22 12:56 ...	XML File	12 KB
readme_parks.txt	2011-08-22 12:56 ...	Text Document	1 KB
TCL3_UPARK.shx	2011-08-22 12:56 ...	SHX File	18 KB
TCL3_UPARK.shp	2011-08-22 12:56 ...	SHP File	1,439 KB
TCL3_UPARK.sbx	2011-08-22 12:56 ...	SBX File	3 KB
TCL3_UPARK.sbn	2011-08-22 12:56 ...	SBN File	24 KB
TCL3_UPARK.prj	2011-08-22 12:56 ...	PRJ File	1 KB
City Green Spaces - EDCT (FGDC) - TCL3...	2011-08-22 12:56 ...	HTML Document	20 KB
TCL3_UPARK.dbf	2011-08-22 12:56 ...	DBF File	225 KB
metadata.css	2011-08-22 12:56 ...	Cascading Style S...	6 KB

Source: Toronto.ca/open; http://www1.toronto.ca/wps/portal/open_data/open_data_home?vgnextoid= b3886aa8cc819210VgnVCM10000067d60f89RCRD.

Figure 4.4. Attribute Information of Parks Shapefile

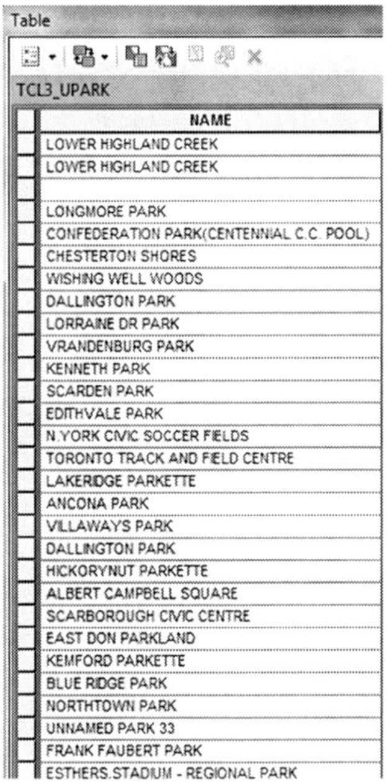

NAME
LOWER HIGHLAND CREEK
LOWER HIGHLAND CREEK
LONGMORE PARK
CONFEDERATION PARK(CENTENNIAL C.C. POOL)
CHESTERTON SHORES
WISHING WELL WOODS
DALLINGTON PARK
LORRAINE DR PARK
VRANDENBURG PARK
KENNETH PARK
SCARDEN PARK
EDITHVALE PARK
N.YORK CIVIC SOCCER FIELDS
TORONTO TRACK AND FIELD CENTRE
LAKERIDGE PARKETTE
ANCONA PARK
VILLAWAYS PARK
DALLINGTON PARK
HICKORYNUT PARKETTE
ALBERT CAMPBELL SQUARE
SCARBOROUGH CIVIC CENTRE
EAST DON PARKLAND
KEMFORD PARKETTE
BLUE RIDGE PARK
NORTHTOWN PARK
UNNAMED PARK 33
FRANK FAUBERT PARK
ESTHERS.STADIUM - REGIONAL PARK

Source: Toronto.ca/open; http://www1.toronto.ca/wps/portal/open_data/open_data_home?vgnextoid=
b3886aa8cc819210VgnVCM10000067d60f89RCRD.

data set is added into a GIS program, it will display multiple polygons, representing the location and boundaries of the parks in Toronto. Along with the visual display of the locations, you also have attribute information available for the shapefile. The attributes can be viewed without a GIS program as well by using a database application, such as Microsoft Excel, to view the .dbf file. Figure 4.4 shows the attributes associated with the shapefile, consisting of the park names. You will learn how to display GIS files in the GIS software section of this chapter.

Geospatial One Stop Geoportal

Geospatial One Stop (GOS) is an American one-stop geoportal for finding and using maps and GIS data. With a large compilation of government data initiatives, and other data resources, GOS offers a collection of GIS data across several themes and categories, such as:

- Administrative boundaries
- Agriculture
- Atmosphere
- Biology
- Business

- Demographic
- Elevation
- Environment
- Health
- Water

Many of these themes are available from multiple resources, from various webpages. GOS doesn't actually host the data but simply provides links to them. So the steps involved in downloading the data will most likely differ from one resource to the next. To get a sense of how GOS works, you will download data from two different sources.

GOS is available from http://gos2.geodata.gov/wps/portal/gos. On the left side of the page, you will find links under Special Interest and links under Data Categories. The first example that will be looked at is under the category of **Agriculture and Farming**. Click on this link available from the left side of the page (Figure 4.5).

Figure 4.5. List of Categories in Geospatial One Stop

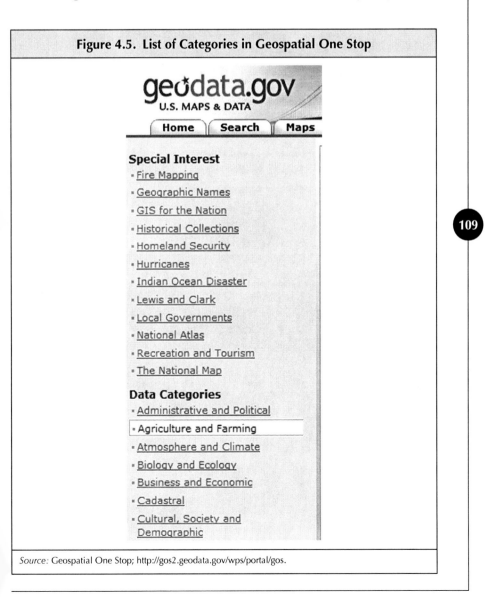

Source: Geospatial One Stop; http://gos2.geodata.gov/wps/portal/gos.

There are two agricultural resources available; however, only one provides GIS data, whereas the second provides an interactive mapping application. The U.S. Department of Agriculture offers data for download from its GIS website. To access this website, click on **Go to Website**, or type in the URL: http://datagateway.nrcs.usda.gov/.

The U.S. Department of Agriculture has a GeoSpatial Data Gateway project whereby it offers data on environmental and natural resources. The Gateway offers a user-friendly way to search by area of interest and then browse and select the available data from the catalog.

To begin, click on the green **Get Data** button. Now you can begin your search for data. In this example you will search for data for certain counties in Arizona. In the State pull-down menu, select **Arizona** and select the first three counties, **Apache**, **Cochise**, and **Coconino**. Add the counties to the Selected List and click **Submit Selected Counties** (Figure 4.6).

Now you should see a list of all the data available for these three counties. Scroll down the list to see what's available, and stop at **Soils**. You're interested in the **Common Resource Areas by State**. Click on the **blue information icon** to learn more about this data set. You will notice there is a detailed abstract of the data set, as well as format type and spatial information. You know from the description that you will be downloading a line file in the shapefile format. The spatial reference is unprojected, in geographic coordinates, using North American

110

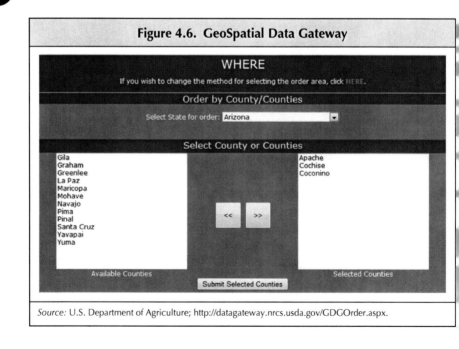

Figure 4.6. GeoSpatial Data Gateway

Source: U.S. Department of Agriculture; http://datagateway.nrcs.usda.gov/GDGOrder.aspx.

Datum 1983 (NAD83). Clicking on the **green plus icon** provides you with a preview of the data set (click on the **eye icon**).

To download this dataset, click on the **box** in front of the data set, and at the bottom of the screen click on **Continue**. There are a number of options for data formats and data projections. Because you're interested in working with shapefiles, select **Esri Shape**. There are a number of projections to select from, but because you won't be working with multiple files, the projection type of this one file doesn't make a difference. If you were in fact working with other files, then the best practice is to try to keep all the files in the same projection. Select the unprojected coordinate system **Geographic NAD83**.

Next, select a delivery method. Because the CD and DVD options cost money, select **FTP**, which is an online download. Click **Continue** at the bottom of the page, where you will be asked to fill out a form with your contact information. An automatic e-mail will be sent to you when the data are ready to be downloaded. The last step is to review the order and, upon acceptance, submit it. You may have noticed that data access from this website was more time consuming and required many more steps than downloading data from the City of Toronto's Open Data website. Every data catalog is different, and sometimes data are available instantly, and other times one needs to wait several hours or days before accessing the data. Because there is no defined protocol or style for these data websites, there is no training manual available for searching and accessing data. What librarians and library users can be trained for, however, is to know how data are normally categorized and what to look for in terms of data formats and spatial reference.

The final example that will be looked at from the GOS is under the category of **Biology and Ecology**. Click on this category, and locate **NatureServe**. NatureServe is a nonprofit conservation organization that provides data on plants and animals for Canada, the United States, and the Western Hemisphere. Access the website by clicking on the link or via this URL: http://www.natureserve.org/aboutUs/index.jsp.

To see the list of available data for download, click on the **Get Data** link available from the top menu. Here you will see a large collection of animal and plant-themed data sets. Read the descriptions of all the data to get a sense of what is available. For this exercise you will examine the **Animal Data**.

Click on **Digital Distribution Maps of Birds of the Western Hemisphere**. All the files are available near the bottom of the page. Even though the website refers to these files as "ArcView" files, they should be labeled as "Shapefiles." ArcView is a specific GIS program, and there are many GIS programs that read shapefiles. You may click on any of the files, unzip them, and examine the contents of the folder. You will find several shapefiles, many of them consisting of points, lines, and polygons. Figure 4.7 shows the **Mimidae** shapefiles displayed in a GIS program.

Figure 4.7. Mimidae Data Set

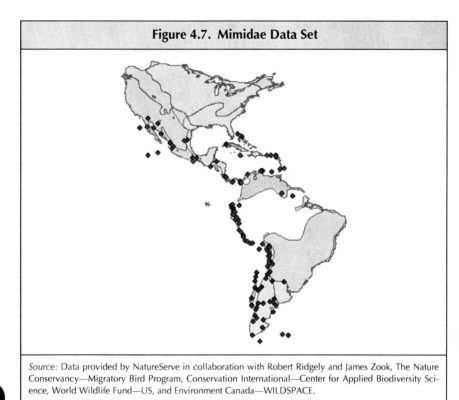

Source: Data provided by NatureServe in collaboration with Robert Ridgely and James Zook, The Nature Conservancy—Migratory Bird Program, Conservation International—Center for Applied Biodiversity Science, World Wildlife Fund—US, and Environment Canada—WILDSPACE.

GIS Software

Because very few online interactive mapping websites support the importation of shapefiles, a proper GIS software program needs to be used to view and manipulate the GIS files to create a map or conduct relational or spatial analysis. One does not need to be an expert in GIS to use these programs. Although they do provide advanced features for GIS users, many library users take advantage of their simple mapping capabilities. Mapping in a GIS program can be as simple as adding the shapefiles, changing the symbology, and adding cartographic elements (legend, north arrow, etc.). There are many GIS programs available, and every few years additional ones appear on the market. There are proprietary desktop programs such as Esri's ArcGIS, and there are also many free open source desktop products available for download from the web. Most recently, GIS applications have also become available online, such as GIS Cloud. The following sections will review some of software programs available.

Esri's GIS Software

The Environmental Systems Research Institute (Esri), founded in 1969, is a software development and services company that develops GIS software and data.

It is the creator of the shapefile format, first introduced in ArcView, version 2, in the early 1990s. In 2009, Esri had approximately 30 percent share of the GIS global market, with an estimated 70 percent of current GIS users using Esri products (*Wikipedia*, 2011). One of Esri's most popular GIS products is ArcGIS, a Windows suite consisting of several applications. ArcMap is one of the applications within the suite and is the mapping program used by most educational institutions and businesses. In September 2010, Esri released ArcGIS version 10, which had been revised considerably from its previous 9.3 version. During searches for data or software, you may see references made to some of Esri's older products such as ArcInfo and ArcView.

ArcGIS is the leading GIS software program purchased by educators. Most academic institutions purchase Esri software licenses, allowing distributions of the software to the academic community. With Esri's strong commitment to educating K to 12, and beyond, online training is available for all levels of expertise. In order for users to utilize GIS software, and for educators to teach with it, it must be easily accessible and user friendly. This is what makes ArcGIS an excellent choice of software for users of all levels. Many GIS librarians value the product and offer their campus community training sessions and workshops.

Esri also offers other GIS solutions to its users. There is a free lightweight version of the GIS program called ArcGIS Explorer. There is also a free web application, ArcGIS Online, that offers data searches and data sharing. Both ArcGIS's ArcMap program and ArcGIS Explorer will be further discussed in the tutorial section of this chapter.

113

Open Source GIS

Open source programs are applications that allow access to the source code. Users can alter the code and use it to create an enhanced product or a new product all together. From a map maker's point of view however, open source products are wonderful alternatives to proprietary software such as ArcMap because the products are almost always free of cost and free of licensing restrictions. Libraries, businesses, and individuals who cannot afford proprietary GIS programs can choose from a large number of open source products that offer similar features. Library users don't need to rely on library copies of GIS products and can simply download them onto their home computers.

There are many open source GIS products available, and they all differ from one another. Many programs will support the common GIS formats and will offer map making tools. But where they differ is in the complexity of tools available. Some programs will offer advanced map making and analysis

Other Open Source GIS Products
- ForestryGIS (fGIS)
  http://www.forestpal.com/fgis.html
- MapWindow GIS
  http://www.mapwindow.org/
- TatukGIS Viewer
  http://www.tatukgis.com/Products/EditorViewer.aspx
- uDig
  http://udig.refractions.net/

features, file conversion utilities, script creations, customized queries, and so forth. Other programs may offer quite the opposite, where the features are so bare bones that one cannot even access the attribute table, edit symbols or colors, view vector and raster files together, or save or print the map. Open source products are often selected based on the project purposes and on the features available in the program. Specific projects require specific tools, and sometimes two or three products need to be used to complete a complex project.

The tutorial will introduce you to Quantum GIS (QGIS), one of the more popular open source products used by novice and expert users. Many educational institutions recommend QGIS as an alternative to ArcGIS.

Cloud-Based GIS

Cloud-based GIS offers a new way to work with GIS technology that eliminates the need for desktop software programs, licensing agreements, and local file collection and organization. Using cloud computing technology, cloud-based GIS is a web-based GIS that can offer desktop-like GIS experiences in any web browser. A product such as GIS Cloud (http://www.giscloud.com/) is a full-featured GIS created primarily for businesses, eliminating their need for a localized GIS service. GIS Cloud offers data storage, easy file sharing, and project management. The services available range from free to premium, with quite a few features being offered at the free level.

Another example of a cloud-based GIS is Esri's ArcGIS Online (http://www.arcgis.com/), a free repository of maps, GIS applications, tools, and data. Some of the applications available include the ArcGIS.com map viewer, a lightweight map viewer that works with data available from ArcGIS.com. A more advanced application is the ArcGIS Explorer Online, which, along with map making tools, also offers location-based presentation tools. ArcGIS Online offers users the ability to share their maps and their data and to create and join groups. Data and projects can then be shared with the groups or the general public.

Although this chapter will not be providing instructions on how to work with cloud-based GIS technology, it is important nevertheless to be aware of this emerging evolutionary style of GIS applications.

GIS Software Tutorials

In this section, you will have the opportunity to work with the GIS programs that are most widely used by schools and libraries. The first program is the lightweight free downloadable program ArcGIS Explorer Desktop, developed by Esri. This product provides an excellent introduction to desktop GIS software and makes an excellent choice of product for users needing a simplified mapping program. The second tutorial will provide an introduction to map making in ArcGIS. Because it is the most widely used GIS software program, having a working knowledge of some of its features will prove to be valuable for many library-related services. You will, however, need to locate a copy of the program to complete this tutorial because it is a licensed product and not freely available. The final software tutorial is for the open source Quantum GIS (QGIS) software program, which is a free download from the web. QGIS is one of the more popular open source GIS products, offering users a complete GIS experience.

ArcGIS Explorer Desktop

ArcGIS Explorer Desktop is a user-friendly GIS viewer that provides exploration, visualization, and spatial information, packaged with ready to use ArcGIS Online base maps and layers. External data can also be added, such as shapefiles, KML/KMZ files and imagery. ArcGIS Explorer Desktop also offers presentation features, enabling users to create dynamic location-based presentations. ArcGIS Explorer Desktop can be downloaded from http://www.esri.com/software/arcgis/ explorer/index.html.

Introduction to the Interface

Open ArcGIS Explorer Desktop. On the left side of the screen is the table of contents, where your map features or layers will be listed. Your tools are available along the top of the page including the following:

- Presentation tool to capture images of map and playing back
- Find tool to find a geographic area by address, place name, or coordinates
  - Directions—Find driving directions between two locations on the map
  - Route—Find route and driving directions between several locations on the map
  - Measure—Measure distance and area
- Create tool
  - Create folders to organize contents of map
  - Create notes on map using a variety of symbols (change color and size from the Appearance folder)
- Map tool
  - Select from a number of base maps
  - Add content—Shapefiles, raster data, KML/KMZ, ArcGIS Online data, and more
  - Analysis—Perform spatial analysis (buffers)
  - 2D/3D—Toggle between the two views

Adding Content

To begin, you're going to explore the variety of data layers that are available in ArcGIS Explorer Desktop. First, examine the type of base maps available. From

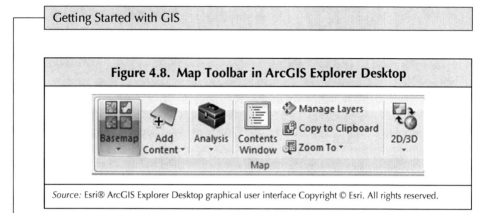

Figure 4.8. Map Toolbar in ArcGIS Explorer Desktop

the Map toolbar, click on **Basemap** (Figure 4.8), and browse the different mapping products. Select the **OpenStreetMap** base map.

You're going to zoom into an area of interest to appreciate the level of detail available. From the **Find** toolbar, click on **Find** and type in **Knoxville, Tennessee.** Click **Enter** on your keyboard to fly to Knoxville. Use the navigation tools on the left side of the map to zoom into the street level. If you like, you can explore different parts of the world as well, as both OpenStreetMap and ArcGIS Explorer Desktop support world coverage.

Next you will add content to your map. ArcGIS Online has a large collection of premade maps that can be added to your map view. From the **Map** toolbar, click on **Add Content**, and then select **ArcGIS Online**. You will see a collection of featured maps that ArcGIS Online is promoting. You can also search for maps of specific locations or themes. In the **Search ArcGIS Online** box, type in the theme **zoning**, and click on the **magnifying glass** to display the results (Figure 4.9). You will see a large collection of zoning and land use maps for different areas of the United States and the world. Find one that you are interested in and click on **Open** so it gets added to your map view.

Next, you will conduct a search based on geographic area. In the search box, type in **New York City**. Select one of the maps, and click **Open**. Because this map will be replacing the zoning map, you will be asked whether you would like to save the previous map. Respond **No**, and your new map will load, deleting your previous zoning map from the table of contents on the left side.

Figure 4.9. Adding Content into ArcGIS Explorer Desktop

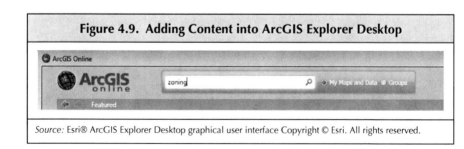

116

As you can imagine, there are thousands of maps available for viewing from ArcGIS Online. However, one certainly isn't limited to using data from just one source. Users can add shapefiles, KML files, as well as text files into their map view.

You will add external files available from the City of Vancouver Open Data Catalogue (http://data.vancouver.ca/datacatalogue/index.htm). Connect to this website and within the data table locate **Business Improvement Areas (BIA)** and download the KML file onto your local computer. Also download the shapefile (.shp) for **Building Footprints 1999**. The Building Footprints file is zipped and will first need to be unzipped before it can be used. Once you have unzipped it, go back to ArcGIS Explorer Online, and add the shapefile (**Add Content, Shapefiles**), and the KML file (**Add Content, KML Files**). Both files will appear in your map view. Because the base map may interfere with the new files, go to **Basemap** and change it from OpenStreetMap to **Bing Maps Aerial**. Now your newly added files should be much more visible.

You can use ArcGIS Explorer Desktop to view any shapefiles and KML/KMZ files that you have access to. You can also add raster data, such as high-resolution aerial photography, text or tabular files with coordinate information, GPS files, image overlays, and more.

Additional features that can be added to the map, such as points, lines, polygons, and other graphics, are available from the **Create** toolbar. Users can add notes or descriptions to these graphics, and they become part of the table of contents. Figure 4.10 shows some of the graphics added to the map view.

117

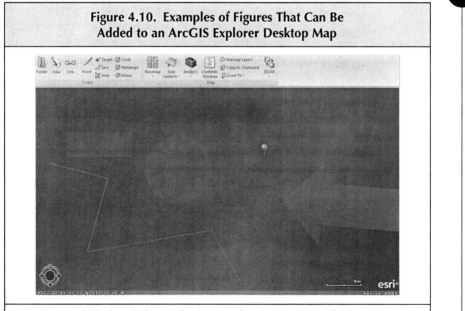

Figure 4.10. Examples of Figures That Can Be Added to an ArcGIS Explorer Desktop Map

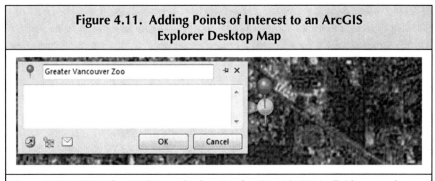

Figure 4.11. Adding Points of Interest to an ArcGIS Explorer Desktop Map

You will now add points of interest to the map. Using the **Find** tool, locate the **Greater Vancouver Zoo**. From the **Create** toolbar, click on the **Point** tool and insert a point over the Greater Vancouver Zoo. Replace the **Note** text with the label **Greater Vancouver Zoo** (Figure 4.11). Now go to the **Appearance** folder and change the red pushpin symbol to another symbol of your choice. Repeat these steps for two other points of interest—the Capilano Suspension Bridge, and Stanley Park.

You should now have a map with three points; a shapefile, a KML file, and an aerial photograph as the basemap. This map can be printed with a title and can be saved as an ArcGIS Explorer Desktop image file. Unfortunately, cartographic elements such as the legend, scale, and north arrow are not available in the final map. Although the product does a fabulous job viewing shapefiles and KML files and connecting to online maps, it really is just a viewer, so file manipulation and data exports are not possible. This product is intended for sharing maps online, not for capturing static maps. Users may create a free account with ArcGIS.com and store all of their maps on that server.

The next Esri product that you will be introduced to, ArcGIS, provides many more map making features and map and file exportation functions. Extending beyond the capabilities of GIS viewers, ArcGIS offers editing, database management, complex analysis, creation of geographic models, and support for a wide range of data types and formats.

Esri's ArcGIS

As has been mentioned earlier in this chapter, ArcGIS is the number one GIS software program used by GIS professionals. Although it is used as a map making program by students, educators, librarians and other professionals, it is in fact much more than a map maker. It helps users find solutions to spatial and analytical problems and offers all the utilities and tools necessary to do so. Even though ArcGIS's full potential is often not recognized by library users, its mapping capabilities are one of the best available on the market and accessible by many academic library users. Those libraries currently without an established Esri software license may wish to consider incorporating one into their library services.

The following tutorial was created to introduce new users to simple mapping in ArcGIS 10. If you are interested in further training, Esri has several online resources to choose from. Esri offers online training sessions, as well as online how-to guides. Many academic libraries share their workshop tutorials online as well. You must have access to a copy of ArcGIS 10 in order to complete the following tutorial.

Downloading Shapefiles

Before you begin mapping, you will need to download some shapefiles to work with. Natural Earth offers public domain map data sets at a variety of scales for the entire world. This tutorial will be working with the cultural vector files, available from Natural Earth's website: http://www.naturalearthdata.com/.

Connect to the Natural Earth website, and click on **Get the Data**. You will see three different sets of scales. You are interested in the most detailed scale, 1:10 million. Click on the **Cultural** link (Figure 4.12).

119

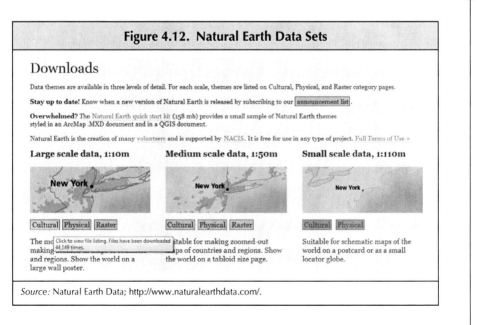

Figure 4.12. Natural Earth Data Sets

Downloads

Data themes are available in three levels of detail. For each scale, themes are listed on Cultural, Physical, and Raster category pages.

Stay up to date! Know when a new version of Natural Earth is released by subscribing to our announcement list.

Overwhelmed? The Natural Earth quick start kit (158 mb) provides a small sample of Natural Earth themes styled in an ArcMap .MXD document and in a QGIS document.

Natural Earth is the creation of many volunteers and is supported by NACIS. It is free for use in any type of project. Full Terms of Use »

Large scale data, 1:10m

Cultural Physical Raster

The mo[st] ... table for making zoomed-out making ... ps of countries and regions. Show and regions. Show the world on a large wall poster.

Medium scale data, 1:50m

Cultural Physical Raster

the world on a tabloid size page.

Small scale data, 1:110m

Cultural Physical

Suitable for schematic maps of the world on a postcard or as a small locator globe.

Source: Natural Earth Data; http://www.naturalearthdata.com/.

Download the following files, and unzip each one so they are ready to work with your GIS program. You will be working with these files for the following QGIS tutorial as well.

- Admin 1—States, Boundaries—Download **States and Provinces** (.shp).
- Populated Places—Download **Populated Places**
- Roads—Download **Roads**
- Railroads—Download **Railroads**
- Urban Areas—Download **Urban Areas**
- Parks and Protected Lands—Download **U.S. National Parks**

Getting Started

ArcGIS has a number of applications packaged together. The mapping software that you will be using is ArcMap. Locate ArcMap on your computer and launch it. A start-up splash window will appear (Figure 4.13). Click **OK**.

Examine the ArcMap interface. You will see the Table of Contents on the left side of the screen. This is where your list of layers will appear. Your drawn layers will display on the larger screen, in the Data View. Your navigation toolbar is available just above the Table of Contents (Figure 4.14). Hover your mouse over these tools to become acquainted with them.

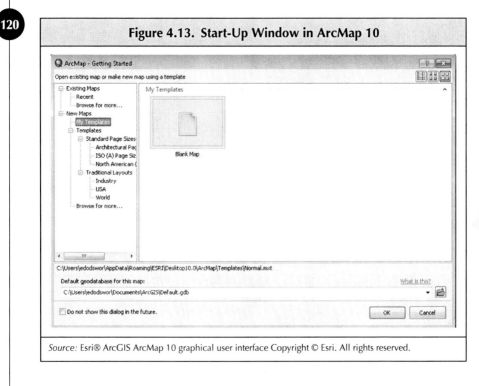

Figure 4.13. Start-Up Window in ArcMap 10

Source: Esri® ArcGIS ArcMap 10 graphical user interface Copyright © Esri. All rights reserved.

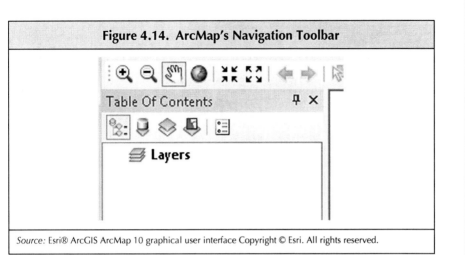

Similarly to ArcGIS Explorer Desktop, ArcMap supports different data types and offers connections to online data. Data can be added to the Data View by clicking on the **Add Data icon** from the toolbar menu, or by going to **File** and **Add Data**. Click on **File** and then **Add Data** and select **Add Basemap**. The list of base maps may be familiar to you. Select the **Bing Maps Aerial** and click on **Add**. You will now have aerial imagery available to you for the entire world. If you like, you can use your zoom tool to zoom into an area of interest. To do so, click on the **zoom tool**, and with your mouse draw a square over the area you would like to zoom into.

Users can also take advantage of the maps available from ArcGIS Online by going to **File, Add Data** and selecting **Add Data from ArcGIS Online**. This will bring you to the large collection of maps that have been explored already with ArcGIS Explorer Desktop.

You will now start adding the GIS files that have been downloaded from Natural Earth. Go back to **File, Add Data**, and select **Add Data.** You will need to connect to the folder that you have saved your shapefiles to. To do this, click on **Connect to Folder** (Figure 4.15), and navigate to the appropriate folder. Click on **Add** and continue clicking on **Add** until you see your collection of shapefiles. Because you have established this connection now, you shouldn't need to connect to the folder again; instead you'll be able to locate your folder and files by pulling down on the **Look in** search box.

You will add each shapefile to your map, one by one. Click on the first folder, click **Add**, and then select the shapefile and **Add** it to your map. To go back to your collection of files to add the next one, click on **Add Data** (either from the file menu or using the toolbar icon), and move up one directory level by clicking on the arrow icon **Up One Level**. You will see your list of features again. Go ahead

121

Figure 4.15. Connecting to Data Folder in ArcMap

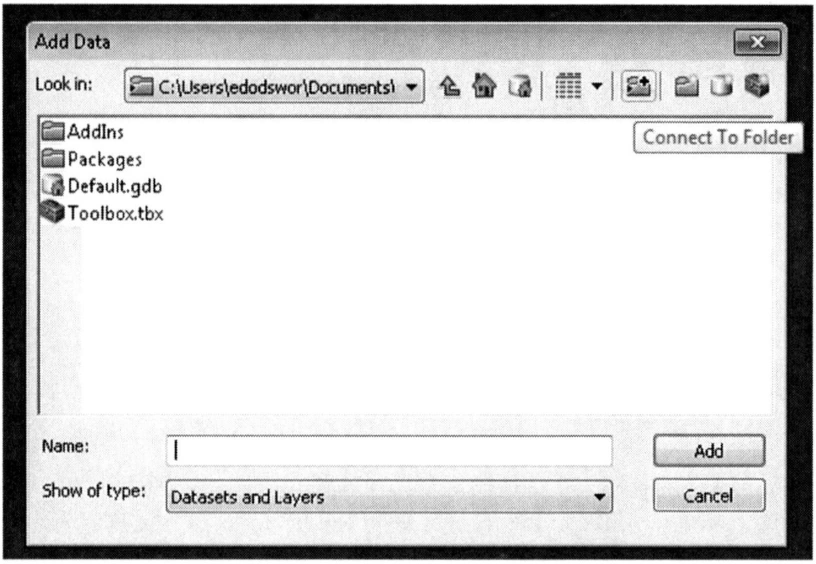

122

and click on the second one, and repeat this until you have added all the shape files to your map. Once completed, your Table of Contents and Map View will look like Figure 4.16.

Although you have data coverage for the entire world, this tutorial will focus on the state of Florida. You will be creating a map of Florida with an additional map inset for Orlando.

Zoom into Florida. You will notice that ArcMap has assigned arbitrary colors to all the features. You will now spend some time adjusting the look of the map by working with the layers' symbology.

Customizing Feature Symbology

The first thing you may notice is that the state boundaries are covering up the Bing Maps Aerial imagery. This is because ArcMap had assigned a solid color to the state boundaries. Locate the State Boundary shapefile in the Table of Contents (10m_admin_1_states_provinces), and double click on its symbol (the **rectangle**). This will bring up the Symbol Selector, allowing you to change the fill color of the states, as well as the outline width and color. Because the aerial imagery needs to remain visible, select the symbol to be **hollow** and change the outline color to **Grey 20%**. Click **OK**.

Figure 4.16. Shapefiles Added and Displayed in ArcMap

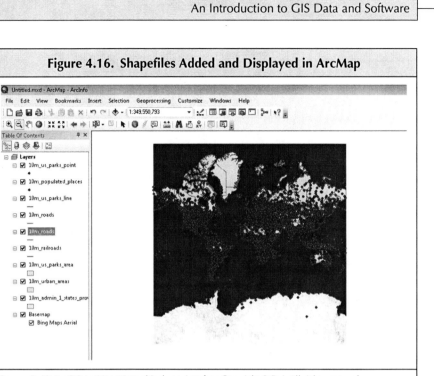

Source: Esri® ArcGIS ArcMap 10 graphical user interface Copyright © Esri. All rights reserved.

Next, you're going to adjust the symbology for the urban areas. Double click on the **10m_urban_areas** file and select the color to be **yellow** and click **OK**. You will add transparency to this layer as well. Right click on the **Properties** layer in the Table of Contents and click on the **Display** folder. In the **transparency** field, type in **50%** (Figure 4.17), and click **OK**.

Figure 4.17. Adjusting Transparency of Layer in ArcMap

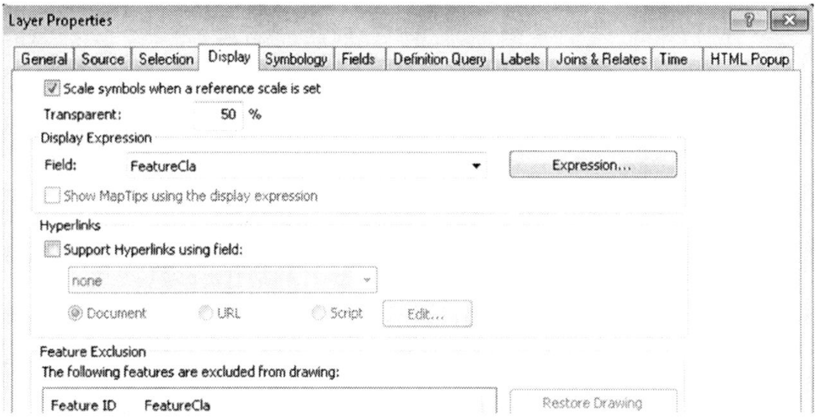

Source: Esri® ArcGIS ArcMap 10 graphical user interface Copyright © Esri. All rights reserved.

For the following three features, apply symbology as follows:

- US Parks_area—Green fill, made 65% transparent; outline color, fir green; line width 2
- Railroads—Railroad line symbol; color, grey 60%; line width 7
- Populated Places—Color, Mars red

Remove the US Park_Point feature from the Table of Contents by right clicking on it and selecting **Remove**. Repeat with the US Park_Line feature.

The last feature that will be customized is the **roads** file. First, examine its attributes to determine how best to symbolize this feature. Right click on the **Roads** shapefile and select **Open Attribute Table**. If you look at the **Type** column, you will see that the roads have been categorized by three types—ferry, major highway, and secondary highway. You will symbolize these so that each category gets its own unique color. Close the attribute table. Right click on the **Roads** shapefile and **Properties**. Click on the **Symbology** folder. On the left side, select **Categories** and **Unique Values**. In the **Value** field, select the attribute that you want to categorize, which is **Type**. Then click on **Add All Values** in order to populate the box (Figure 4.18). Click **OK**.

Figure 4.18. Displaying Attribute Categories by Symbol in ArcMap

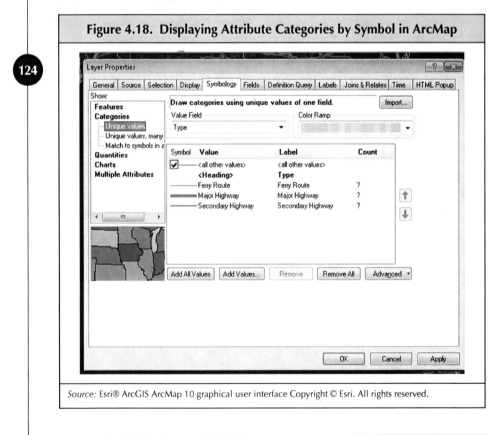

To customize the color of each transportation line, you will need to double click on each one to assign a width and a color. Double click on the **Major Roads** symbol in the Table of Contents. Select the **Highway** style line, and decrease the line width to 2. Click on the **Secondary Roads** symbol and select the **Major Road** style line, and change the line color to **Electron Gold**. We will leave the Ferry symbol as is.

Now that the feature symbols have been organized, map labeling will be worked on next.

Applying Labels

Labels can be applied manually, by adding text over features, or by using the automatic labeling function, which labels features using the information available from the attribute table. You will be adding labels to the parks, but it would be much easier if park names were already available from the attribute tables. To determine whether they are or not, open and examine the Parks attribute table (right click to open the attribute table).

When you examine the table, you will notice there are several populated columns, with the last one providing users with the names of the parks. Now that you know the information is available from this table, take advantage of it and use it to label the parks. The simplest way to label the parks is to right click on the **Parks** shapefile and select **Label Features**. Zoom into the two parks at the southern tip of Florida. You will see that although the parks have been labeled, they are rather difficult to see. Label customization is available from the layer properties.

Right click on the **Parks** shapefile and go to **Properties**. Click on the **Labels** folder. This is where you select the column that you would like to use for labeling the parks, as well as for applying customized label styles. What you want to do here is to increase the font size and apply a mask to the text so that it stands out considerably. Increase the font size to **11** points. To apply the mask, you will need to follow these steps:

- Click on **Symbol**
- Click on **Edit Symbol**
- Click on the **Mask** folder
- Select **Halo**
- Click **OK** on all the windows until they have closed down

What you should see now are very prominent labels for all of the parks (Figure 4.19).

Next you're going to manually add a label to the built up area of Orlando. Locate Orlando and zoom into the area at a scale of approximately 1:700,000. The scale feature in the toolbars allows users to input specific scales. Click on the

125

**Figure 4.19. Parks Prominently Labeled
Using the Mask Feature in ArcMap**

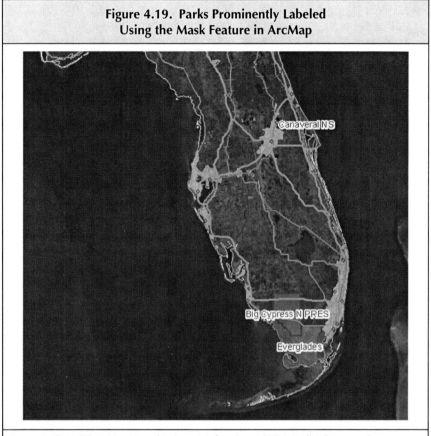

Canaveral NS

Big Cypress N PRES

Everglades

126

Insert menu and select **Text**. Type **Orlando** and press **Enter.** You can now drag the text over the urban area. To customize the text, double click on it to open its properties, and select **Change Symbol**. On the left side, there are several preset label styles. Select **Country2** and then a color of your choice. Click **OK** when finished.

Creating an Inset Map

You have completed the first map. Next you are going to create a map inset of Orlando. To do this, you will need to create a new Data Frame and add the files that you would like displayed. The new Data Frame is like a separate map project all together. To add the new data frame go to the **Insert** menu and select **Data Frame**. Your new Data Frame will be placed below your original collection of files and is now the active one. To switch between Data Frames, simply right click on the Data Frame you would like to activate and select **Activate**. The inset map will be a fairly detailed map of Orlando, with local streets. To achieve this, all you need to do is to add the OpenStreetMap base map to the new map view. Go to **File**, **Add Data**, and select **Add Basemap**. Select **OpenStreetMap** and add it to the view. Zoom into Florida and locate Orlando. Zoom in enough so that you can see the local roads.

To put the two maps together, you will need to switch to Layout View, where you add the final touches to your map. Layout View is accessible from the **View** menu. Once you have changed views, you will notice that both maps are on top of each other. Each map is part of its own frame, so you can easily drag the inset map out of the way, and resize both maps.

First, drag the Orlando map to the southwest corner of the page by selecting the map and dragging it with the mouse. You can adjust the size by moving any of the four corners of the map. You can modify the larger map the same way. At this point you can also adjust the zoom of either map so that your area of interest is displayed within the extent of the map page. If you need to adjust any labels, you can do that as well. Leave some white space on the page to make room for cartographic elements. Your map may look similar to Figure 4.20.

127

Figure 4.20. Map of Florida and Inset Map of Orlando Displayed in ArcMap's Layout View

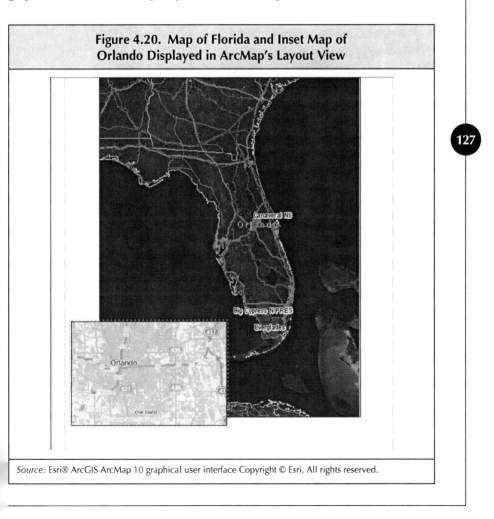

Adding Cartographic Elements

The final touches of map creation are very easy with ArcMap. You can add several cartographic elements to the map, such as title, scale, north arrow, legend, and additional text as well. All of these are available from the Insert menu. Click on **Insert** and select **Title**. Provide a title for your map, such as **Cultural Map of Florida**. The text will be added to your map. You will need to adjust the text location by dragging it to your preferred location. Some map makers like to have titles at the top, and others like to place it near their legend. If you like, you can change the font type, color, and size by double clicking on it and accessing the symbol properties.

Before you add your legend to the map, you may want to clean up the layer names a bit, as the way they are currently labeled is the way they will be displayed in the legend. Double click on each layer label in the Table of Contents. The properties window will pop up. Go to the **General** tab to access the layer name. Replace the current layer name with one that is shorter. For example, you may wish to change 10m_us_parks_area to just simply Parks. Do this for all of the layers. When you're satisfied with the look of the layer labels, you are ready to insert your legend.

From the **Insert** menu, select **Legend**. You will want to include all layers in the legend, so accept the default layers. There are several legend styles available. Click on **Style** to view what's available and to select your preferred style. Click **Next**. If you wish to add a subtitle to your map or a legend title, you can add it under the **Legend Title**. You also have the option to customize the font type, color, and size of it. Click **Next**. If you like you can add a border, background color, and a drop shadow color to your legend. After you have made your choices, click **Next**. Accept the default symbol patch and click **Next**, and then click **Finish**. Your legend has been added to your map. Drag your legend to a vacant area on your map and resize it if necessary (click and drag the corners).

The scale bar will be added next. From the **Insert** menu, select **Scale Bar**. Choose a scale bar, and click on **Properties** to select the units you would like your scale to be displayed in. Click **OK** and drag the scale bar to a preferred location on your map.

To add a north arrow, select it from the **Insert** menu and add it to your map. You will also need to add a citation to your map. From the **Insert** menu select **Text**, and type **GIS Vector Files courtesy of Natural Earth (http://www.naturalearthdata.com/), Basemaps courtesy of Bing Maps Aerial and OpenStreetMap**.

If you wish to add any additional textual elements, you can select them from the **Insert** menu, and choose **Dynamic Text**. You will find a wide range of additional map-related text you can add to your map. When you have completed adding the final touches to your map, it may look similar to Figure 4.21.

Figure 4.21. Completed Map in ArcMap

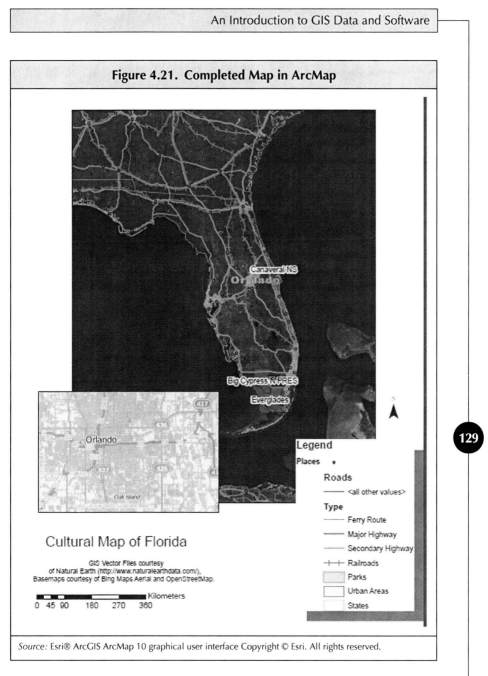

Cultural Map of Florida

GIS Vector Files courtesy
of Natural Earth (http://www.naturalearthdata.com/),
Basemaps courtesy of Bing Maps Aerial and OpenStreetMap.

Legend

Places •

Roads
——— <all other values>

Type
——— Ferry Route
— — — Major Highway
——— Secondary Highway
—+—+— Railroads
☐ Parks
☐ Urban Areas
☐ States

Kilometers
0 45 90   180   270   360

Saving and Printing

If at any time you would like to save your progress and return to your map project later, select **Save** or **Save As** from the **File** menu. When you go back to open your ArcMap project later, you will be able to access it by locating it via the splash screen (the welcome page when you start ArcMap) or by double clicking on the .mxd file. To save your actual map, click on **Export** from the **File** menu. You will have a wide range of image options to choose from. You have the ability to increase or decrease image resolution as well.

To print the map, select **Print** from the **File** menu. If at any time you wish to change your page orientation, you may do so, although you will need to readjust both map frames and zoom levels. Page orientation options are available from **Page and Print Setup**.

This chapter has offered a basic overview of simple map making in ArcGIS. To learn about more features available and to access additional guides, visit the **companion website (http://www.neal-schuman.com/gis)**.

Quantum GIS (QGIS) Version 1.6

QGIS is a free open source GIS program available for Windows, Mac OS X, and Linux. The product can be downloaded from the Quantum GIS Download page at http://www.qgis.org/wiki/Download. The following tutorial will offer a basic introduction to mapping in QGIS, version 1.6. However, you are encouraged to refer to the comprehensive user guide available online at http://www.qgis.org/en/documentation/manuals.htm for a complete overview of the features and programs available in this GIS product.

Getting Started

After you have successfully installed QGIS, start the program. You will notice a common GIS application look and feel:

- Tables of Contents are on the left side of the program.
- Navigation tools are just above the map view.
- Layers can be added using the set of icons above the navigation tools.
- Maps can be saved and printed from the File menu (please save often, as QGIS is known to shut down unexpectedly at times).

You will begin by adding the same shapefiles that you had worked with in the ArcGIS tutorial—the files downloaded from Natural Earth. To add these files, click on the **Add Vector Layer icon** available from the data toolbar (Figure 4.22).

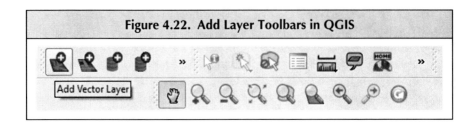

Figure 4.22. Add Layer Toolbars in QGIS

Browse to the folder where your shapefiles are stored and add each shapefile, one by one. Use the **Zoom in** tool to zoom into Florida. Next you will customize the feature symbols.

Customizing Feature Symbology

To compare and contract QGIS's usability to ArcMap's, you will be creating a map using the same features and symbols. First, you will begin by making the state boundary layer hollow. Locate the state boundary layer in the Table of Contents and double click on it to open the symbology properties. Click on the **Fill Options** and then on **None**. Leave the outline the way it is, and click **OK** (Figure 4.23).

Next, symbolize the urban areas. Select a **pink fill**, and adjust the transparency level, available at the top of the screen, to **50%**. Change the outline color to match the fill. Next, customize these layers in the following way:

- Railroads—Select a dash line, colored grey
- Populated Places—Small red star
- US_Parks_area—Green fill, 65% transparency, outline color to match the fill
- US_Parks_point and US_Parks_line—Remove by right clicking on each layer and select **Remove**

131

Figure 4.23. Symbology Properties in QGIS

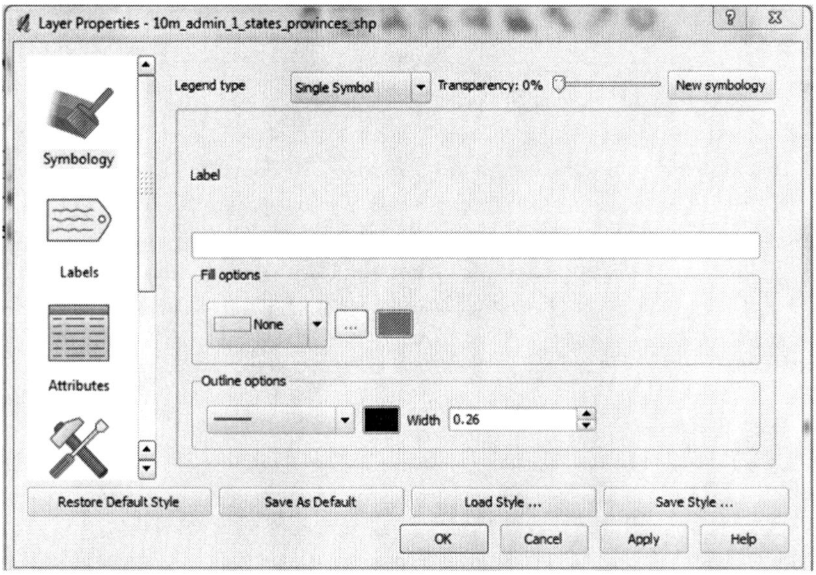

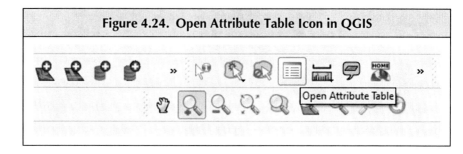

Figure 4.24. Open Attribute Table Icon in QGIS

You will need to categorize the roads layer by the different road types. First, open the roads attribute table to see which column should be categorized. To open the attribute table, select the **Roads** layer in the Table of Contents, and click on the **Open Attribute Table icon** available from the top toolbars (Figure 4.24).

The Roads attribute table will open and you will see that the Type category is the one you want to work with. You will create three symbols for the Roads, one for each road type. To do this, double click on the **Roads** layer to open the Symbology properties. In the **Legend Type**, select **Unique Value**, and in the **Classification Field**, select **Type**. Click on **Classify**. You will now have the three class types listed. To change the symbology colors, click on each symbol and alter the colors and line widths. Click on the **Major Highway** layer, change it to red, and change the line width to 0.50. Then click on the **Secondary Highway** layer, change it to gold, and change the line width to 0.35. Leave the Ferry symbol as is.

Adding base maps to QGIS is possible by connecting to a Web Mapping Service (WMS). To access an aerial view of Florida, follow these steps:

1. In the **Layer** menu, select **Add WMS Layer**.
2. Click on **Add Default Servers**.
3. From the pull-down menu select **Lizardtech server**.
4. Click on **Connect** to access all of the individual layers.
5. One of several sources of imagery is the bmng.200401 file. Click on that file and select **Add**.
6. The image will appear at the top of the Table of Contents, covering all of your data, so click on the file and drag it to the bottom of the list.

Your map should look similar to Figure 4.25.

Adding Labels

QGIS will label features based on information available from the attribute table, and it also supports user-added text for customized labeling. You will be labeling all of the Populated Places using the names supplied from the Populated Places attribute table. Open the **Populated Places** attribute table to determine which column should be used for labeling. Upon examination of the table you will see

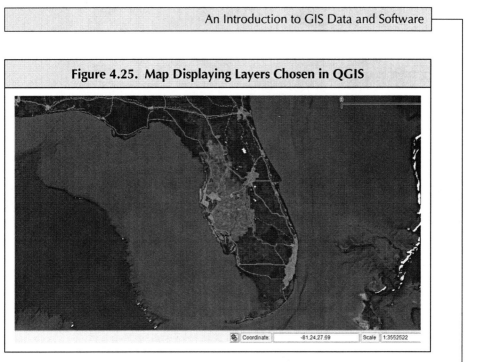

Figure 4.25. Map Displaying Layers Chosen in QGIS

that the **Name** column is the one that you are interested in. Double click on the **Populated Places** layer to open **Layer Properties**. On the left side you will see a list of properties, one of them being Labels. Select **Labels** and click on **Display Labels**. Because the column you will be labeling is the Name column, select **Name** from the **Field Containing Name** drop box. You would like the labels to appear not over the icons, but just above, so under **Placement** select **Above**. Change the color of the font to red, and keep the font type and size as is. When you have finished, click **OK** to see your labeled map.

Adding Finishing Touches

QGIS has additional features available that will assist in completing your map. These features need to be enabled first, however. Under the **Plugins** menu, select **Manage Plugins**. Select the following plug-ins and then click **OK**:

- North Arrow
- OpenStreetMap
- Scale Bar

The North Arrow and Scale Bar plug-ins will be present in Print mode. The OpenStreetMap plug-in will provide a connection to OpenStreetMap vector data. To see how this works, you will need to zoom into a fairly small area of Orlando, as it has limitations on the size coverage. Zoom into the Urban Area of Orlando, and adjust the scale bar at the bottom right of the program to read 1:15,000. Turn off the Urban Area layer from the Table of Contents. You will notice a new set

133

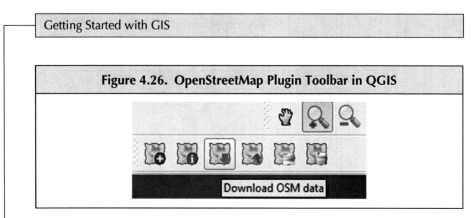

Figure 4.26. OpenStreetMap Plugin Toolbar in QGIS

of toolbars just above the map. Click on **Download OSM Data** (Figure 4.26). Select a folder on your local computer where the data can be saved to and click **Download**.

It may take a couple of minutes for OpenStreetMap data to appear; when it does, zoom out a bit to see the full extent of the data. OpenStreetMap layers also have attribute information associated with them, so, if you like, you may also label some of the new features. Now you're ready to add the finishing touches to the map.

The labels on the legend items need to be improved for legibility. Provide each layer with an appropriate name by double clicking on each one and accessing the **General** properties. There you will have the ability to rename all the layers appropriately.

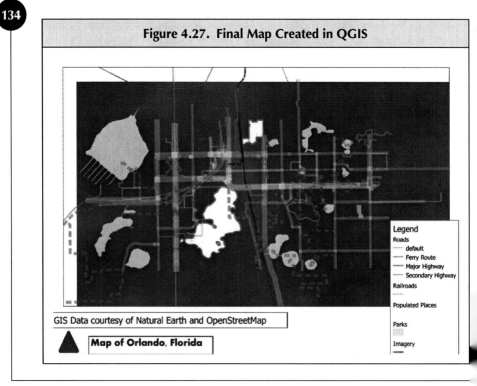

Figure 4.27. Final Map Created in QGIS

Building the final map is done in the Print Composer. Select **New Print Composer** from the **File** menu. You will see an empty canvas with several mapping tools available from the Layout menu. Anything selected from the Layout menu can be edited from the Item folder on the far right of the program. Select the **Layout** menu, and click on **Add Map**. Using your mouse, draw the extent of map coverage you would like to have on your canvas. Then add the **Vector Legend** by clicking on the location of the map where you would like it displayed. In the **Item** folder, you can edit the legend to remove raster layers because it is only a vector legend. Next, from the **Layout** menu, select **Add Label**. Your text font type, size, and color can be modified from the Item menu as well. Repeat these steps with anything else you would like to add to your map. When finished, you can save your map by selecting **File** and then **Export**. Figure 4.27 is an example of what your final map may look like.

Conclusion

You have now completed several tutorials using different GIS products. If your mapping needs are satisfied with viewers such as ArcGIS Explorer Desktop or open source QGIS, then you can easily install these programs on library computers and create how-to guides for library users. Although all GIS programs differ in terms of mapping features and levels of functionality, the underlying principles of mapping remains the same in all GIS programs. When library staff begin looking at GIS programs to use for digitization or georeferencing projects, then the array of software options becomes much smaller. As you will see in Chapters 5 and 6, ArcGIS is used in some libraries for purposes beyond simple mapping, and, because of this, many libraries do in fact prefer to work with ArcGIS over free products that can be somewhat limiting.

This chapter has also introduced you to the fundamental principles of GIS data, data collections, and data retrieval. With this newly gained knowledge, you may find yourself much more comfortable recommending data resources and answering data-related reference questions. Although this chapter has focused on using GIS software programs for viewing and mapping shapefiles, you should also know that there are ways to use shapefiles without necessarily needing to use a GIS program. Sometimes when library users are not comfortable working with GIS files, it may be beneficial for them to limit themselves to something they are more comfortable with—working with Google Earth and KML files. Although most GIS data are not yet available in KML format, it is possible to convert shapefiles to KML files. This will be discussed in detail in Chapter 5.

Reference

Wikipedia. 2011. "ESRI." *Wikipedia.* Last modified February 15. http://en.wikipedia.org/wiki/Esri.

135

Opening Access to Collections with Geodigitization Projects

Introduction: Opening Access to Library Collections

Libraries hold large collections of books, photographs, newspapers, music, maps, archival material, and much more. Access to these materials is often available by visiting the holding library. Common collections are available in the stacks, but often restricted or specialized materials are accessible only in segmented rooms, with limited hours. Some material can be accessed only via a staff person with a premade appointment. Sometimes the material needs to be handled with additional caution, with prohibitions against being scanned or copied. Nontraditional materials such as historical photographs, diaries, postcards, and air photos may be difficult for the inexperienced library user to find. Indexes and search aids exist, but quite often there are different indexes for every product, making access to the collection potentially very time consuming and challenging.

Arguably, books and journals are one of the easiest types of library materials to locate. They have been cataloged and placed in a call number sequence on library shelves. Yet, many libraries are now opting to purchase digital versions of these types of collections. So, in many cases, digital access to material is offered to library users not because the material is difficult to access but because it is more convenient to access without needing to step away from the computer. If books and journals can be accessed digitally by users, then perhaps it's time for libraries to also consider digitizing some of their harder to access collections. Easier access of course has the benefit of increased usage. When hard-to-find and difficult-to-access material becomes easily available and accessible, then users who in the past couldn't visit the library during restricted hours will now have access to not only the materials they were specifically looking for but also to material they didn't know existed.

137

This chapter will review several libraries that have digitized their specialized collections to make the material not only accessible online but also easy to locate using GIS technology. This chapter also includes tutorials for how to use applications to geotag material with a locational component, as well as convert spatial files into the KML format.

Geodigitizing Content in Libraries

Information can be searched online in a couple of different ways—textually or spatially. One can use text to enter subject information into a database, like Google, or one can use a map to locate information based on location, like Google Maps. If the location of a resource is important, then having the resource made available through a map index may be the best way to provide access to this type of location-based resource. For example, if users are interested in obtaining information about a specific neighborhood or city, then using an online mashup created with Google Maps may be the most successful way to promote and deliver the library's collection that includes resources for that specific geographic area.

Of course not all library material can be cataloged by geography, but some key resources certainly can: postcards, photographs, historical documents like diaries and newspaper clippings, books and stories, air photos, and GIS data sets, to name a few. If your library has a collection with a significant geographic element, you may want to consider using GIS technology to expose and deliver this collection.

One of the more popular ways of exposing collections to the public is using online map mashups. You may recall from previous chapters that map mashups are created by geotagging, or embedding coordinate information into a placemark, document, or an image. This is often done with user-friendly programs such as Google Earth, Flickr, Picasa, or Zooomr. Georeferencing images and sharing them online is also becoming a popular way to showcase and distribute collections.

Distributing Library Content with Map Mashups

Mapping technology has greatly influenced the ways libraries are offering collection search, discovery, and distribution methodology and tools. Many libraries are combining location and relevant library material to create map mashups in applications like Google Earth, Google Maps, and Bing Maps, to name a few. These map mashups offer an easy way to search for and access digitized library material based on the resources' geographic locations. Not only do the mapping applications offer an innovative way to search for material, but the applications themselves may be considered by many library users to be a more popular and user-friendly search "catalogs" over the traditional library ones (Markey, 2007).

138

Any number of resources can be added to a map mashup. Popular online collections include images, maps, documents, books, and archival materials like diaries, postcards, and photographs and in fact anything else available in the library's collection. Books about specific geographic locations can easily be organized and found using a spatial or map catalog. Although using mapping technology as an interface to the library's catalog is just beginning to gain popularity among libraries, the first signs of this innovative location-based approach started occurring several years ago.

In 2005, the Portland State University Library digitized a large number of planning documents, including literature, planning reports, maps, images, and geographical data. Access to these collections was made available from the library catalog. However, to increase the exposure of this project, access to the catalog was also made available via Google Earth. Placemarks were created in Google Earth to represent specific locations. Then collection details were added, such as the title and description of the collection, texts, and URLs for the collection-specific links and related images. When users click on the placemark, all relevant library resources for that one location become available. This project has offered users easy distribution of library material in a fun and attractive way, as well as easy collection sharing with transportability with KML files (Brenner and Klein, 2008).

The use of Google mapping technology to point to information available in another location, such as a website or a library catalog, will certainly provide an additional point of access to the library's collection. The Kingston Public Library, in Ontario, created a pilot project using Google Maps as an interface to certain bibliographic records in its catalog. With Google Maps API, the project consisted of placemark links to relevant search results in the library's catalog. Markers were available at the country level for specific subjects of history and travel, and clicking on the marker prompted a search for bibliographic records related to the country and theme selected (Vandenburg, 2008).

More recently, both public and academic libraries in North America have shown a lot of interest in using mapping technology to showcase and distribute their library collections. Many are map mashups created using Google Maps, where placemarks are created and additional library information is made available through links within the placemark. A typical example of this type of project work is the University of Vermont Library's digitized Long Trail Collection (University of Vermont, 2011). Over 900 images of the oldest long-distance hiking trail in the United States have been scanned and geotagged in Google Maps. Placemarks have been added into Google Maps, with each placemark representing one photograph in the collection. Clicking on the placemark will lead users to the actual photograph, including a description of the photograph and a link to the item's catalog. The map mashup has been embedded into the University of Vermont Library's webpage.

Several map libraries have been sharing their map and air photo collections using map mashups as well. With every placemark representing an air photo, users can click on a placemark over or near their geographic area of interest and have instant access to an air photo representing that area. University of Western Ontario's Serge A. Sauer Map Library (University of Western Ontario, 2010) distributes its historical 1922 air photos of London, Ontario, this way.

Some libraries have also opted to use KML files as a format for resource distribution. Libraries have digitized their collections and converted the image files to the popular KML format. These files can be downloaded and viewed in Google Earth and Google Maps, as well as easily shared with others. KML files can either be geotagged or georeferenced and in the library setting often consist of air photos, maps, and GIS data.

In fact, several libraries have converted their GIS shapefiles into KML files to broaden the user base, knowing that Google Earth is a more popular application among non-GIS users. One example is the University of Connecticut Library (2011), which provides GIS data in a number of formats, including KML. Converting shapefiles to KML files is a fairly easy process and will be discussed in the tutorial section of this chapter.

As discussed in previous chapters, map mashups are popular among libraries for noncollection uses, such as for directions and library locations. Public libraries may find map mashups particularly useful in answering common reference questions such as the locations of local landmarks. The Franklin Park Public Library, in Illinois, has generated a map of city landmarks. Using customized icons for the placemarks, it has also included place name, website URL of the organization, and, when possible, an image of the location (Jacobsen, 2008). All images that are embedded into Google Maps or Google Earth need to be linked to an online server; several image storage sites available online will be discussed in the tutorial section as well.

Creating Map Mashups and Geodigitizing Library Collections: Tutorials

This section will provide an overview of some of the tools available online that can be used in creating a map interface for the organization and/or the delivery of library collections. The key components to geodigitization projects include the creation, organization, and compilation of resources, identifying their geographic locations, and mounting the resources on a mapping interface accessible by the public.

The first set of tutorials will include methodology for creating resource distribution map mashups, including the uploading of images to an image server, the development and geocoding of resources, and the creation of the final map mashup. The second set of tutorials will review applications and utilities that convert shapefiles to KML files, expanding the GIS user base and braiding Google Maps technology into the library's resources and culture. Georeferencing techniques will also be briefly discussed.

Digitizing Library Collections

Before any resources can be shared with library users online, they must first be made available electronically. For those wishing to use map mashups as a link to the library catalog, no further digitization is required. However, for projects that involve converting paper to digital, a proper scanning process and an image hosting website are both essential.

The resolution that documents and images should be scanned at will depend on the quality and size of the output desired. Large files are not recommended for the web, because they take up server space and will take longer for the users to download. For archival quality, documents are normally scanned at 600 dpi and saved in the .tif image file format. For web-quality digitization projects, however, it's best to scan images at about 72 to 96 dpi and save as .jpg images. Increasing the dpi will increase the resolution of the digital image, so it may be best to experiment with the number of dpi first.

After documents have been scanned and saved, they need to be uploaded to a web server to make them accessible online. Libraries often have the server space available to host a large number of images, but if that is not the case, you may want to take advantage of free image hosting services such as Flickr (http://www .flickr.com/) or Picasa (http://picasa.google.com/). Once you have uploaded your images to the website, every image is given its own URL address, allowing you to easily provide the link on your Google Map. Alternatively, one can also embed the actual image in Google Maps or Google Earth, so, instead of using a link to the image, the actual image itself will be visible when users click on the placemark. This can easily be done by using Picasa, which also offers an excellent geocoding utility.

Geocoding Digital Projects in Picasa

Picasa is a free photo organizer, photo viewer, and editing tool from Google, offering users the ability to also geotag the photos on Google Maps or Google Earth. Photos can be stored and shared online with Picasa Web Albums. Picasa does, however, require an install, because the organization of files is done on the local computer and then uploaded online to the Picasa Web Albums. Taking advantage of the online album will require a Google account.

To begin, go to http://picasa.google.com/ and install Picasa. Once installed, launch Picasa and upload your images into the program. To geotag your images so that they are accessible outside of Picasa, you will first need to select all of the

Figure 5.1. Geotag Icon in Picasa

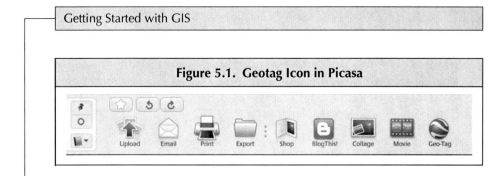

Figure 5.2. Geotag Tool in Google Earth

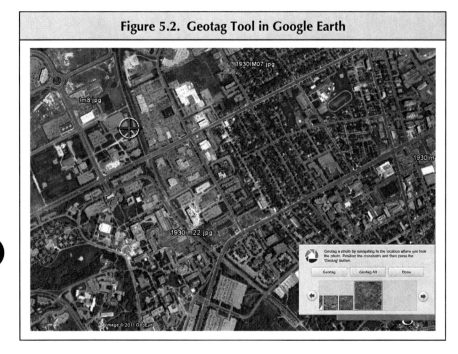

images that require geocoding. Then click on the **Geotag icon** at the bottom of the screen (Figure 5.1). This will launch Google Earth (assuming you have it installed on your computer). Navigate and zoom to the location in Google Earth that corresponds to each image, place the yellow cross-hairs on your chosen location, and click the **Geotag** button to place the selected photo (Figure 5.2).

Repeat this for all of the images you would like to geocode. Once completed, your images will appear in the Table of Contents on the left side of Google Earth, grouped together under the folder entitled **My Picasa Pictures**. At this point, if you wish to add any more information to the images, you can right click on each individual image file from the Table of Contents and in the description box add additional text or links (Figure 5.3). If you're familiar with HTML code, you can embed advanced labels, videos, and other links as well. When users click on the photo, they will see all the information you have included (Figure 5.4).

Figure 5.3. Photo Description Box in Google Earth

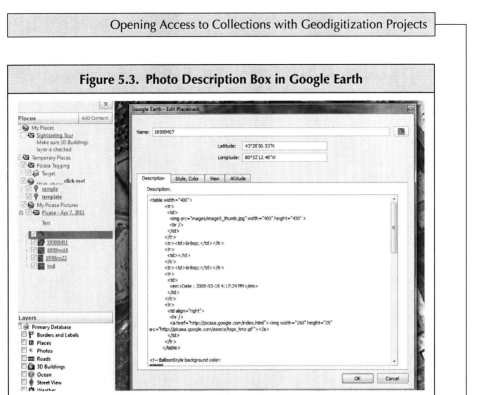

Figure 5.4. Photo Properties in Google Earth

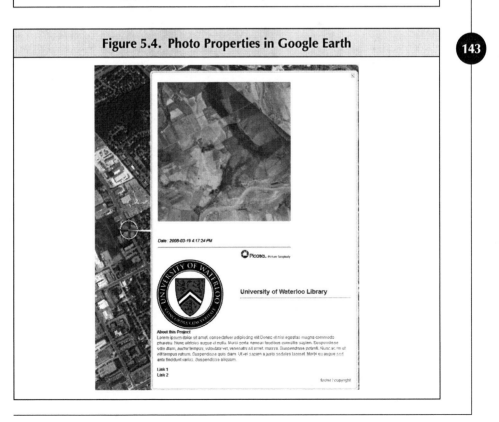

Figure 5.5. Map Mashup of a Digital Collection in Google Earth

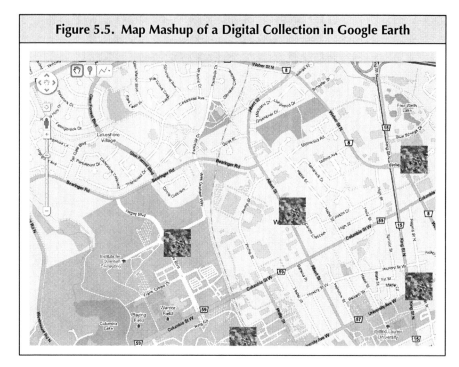

To save all of the images as one KML file, right click on the folder and then **Save Place As,** and save the KML file to your computer. You can share your entire library collection of digitized and geotagged images with others by sending them this one KML file. You can also import your KML file into Google Maps to make a mashup that can be embedded into your library website. Your final map mashup might look similar to Figure 5.5.

Creating Library Collection Map Mashups

Map mashups can be as simple as adding information and links to placemarks on a map. As was discussed in previous chapters, map mashups can be created in a variety of different mapping programs; however, because of the popularity of Google Maps among library users, this map mashup tutorial will be demonstrating Google Maps mashups.

As was outlined in Chapter 3, Google Maps mashups can be easily created using Google Maps' My Maps application. Placemarks can be added to specific geographic locations, and descriptions can be embedded into the placemarks so that when users click on it, a text box pops up populated with resources. When there are quite a few placemarks to add, however, it may be worthwhile to consider using a geocoding application to help map the points in Google Maps. Instead of manually adding each individual point, the application will read the geographic information available from a table and map all rows of information as individual points on the map. As with any placemark that is to be added onto the map, the user will need to know the location of the placemark—the street address or city, depending on the level of detail required. One online application that does an excellent job geocoding a list of addresses is BatchGeo (http://batchgeo.com/).

BatchGeo will take a collection of addresses along with associated information related to the addresses (links and descriptions) and map them in Google Maps. It will also generate a KML file that can be opened in Google Earth, allowing the user to add any additional information to the placemarks, if necessary.

In the following tutorial you will be creating a sample map mashup for the purposes of distributing a library digitization project. Consider your own library collection and what could be geodigitized and included in the placemarks—perhaps links to scanned images, links to the library catalog, and a description of other supporting documents available for the subject being mapped.

Getting Started

To begin, you will need to gather all the library resources that you would like to be made available to the public. Which geographic areas are you representing? In most cases, library collections represent geographic areas at the city level; however, if you have documents that pertain to specific addresses, ensure you have the street name and number of those addresses. In your Excel table, create columns for the following:

- Street name and number
- City
- Province or state
- Postal code (if you know it), but not necessary
- Description of the resource
- Any other information desired (perhaps a link to an image or another document)

Then populate the columns with the information that you have. Figure 5.6 shows a sample table of the information available about a hypothetical digital library project. In order for Google Maps to place each row of information onto a map in the correct location, the address information provided in the table will need to be geocoded in BatchGeo so that it includes latitude and longitude coordinates.

Figure 5.6. Sample Table of Information That Will Be Made Available from a Placemark Icon in Google Maps

	A	B	C	D	E	F	G	
1	Street Address	City	Province	Description	URL	Additional Information	Additional Information	KML
2								
3	King Street South	Kitchener	Ontario	Air photo 1930	http://www.li	Fire Insurance Plans availabl	Historical Atlas availabl	http://www.lib.uwat
4	Bridge Street East	Kitchener	Ontario	Air photo 1930	http://www.li	Fire Insurance Plans availabl	Historical Atlas availabl	http://www.lib.uwat
5	Plains Road	Kitchener	Ontario	Air photo 1945	http://www.li	Fire Insurance Plans availabl	Historical Atlas availabl	http://www.lib.uwat
6	McGarry Drive	Kitchener	Ontario	Air photo 1947	http://www.li	Fire Insurance Plans availabl	Historical Atlas availabl	http://www.lib.uwat

145

Figure 5.7. Validate Geographic Columns in BatchGeo

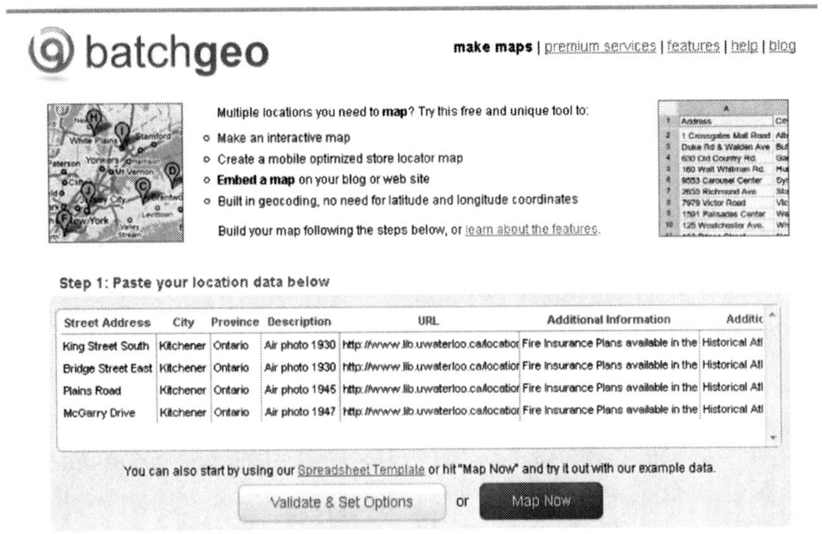

Source: BatchGeo; http://www.batchgeo.com/.

Geocoding in BatchGeo

Connect to the BatchGeo website (http://batchgeo.com/). Follow the steps outlined on the website. The first step is to insert the tabular information you need geocoded into the space provided. To do this, select and copy your Excel columns and rows contents and paste them into BatchGeo. Click on **Validate & Set Options** to match your geographic columns to theirs (Figure 5.7).

Go ahead and validate all the column information and then progress to Step 3. Click on **Make Google Map**. Your information will be geocoded instantly and made available in Google Maps. Each row is now represented as a placemark (Figure 5.8).

Currently, the map is available only online from BatchGeo's website. In order to extract the map as a KML file so that further editing and sharing can be done, you will need to proceed to the next step, which is saving the map. Click

> **Geocoding with Google Fusion Tables**
>
> BatchGeo is certainly not the only online product available for geocoding lists of addresses. Google's own Google Fusion Tables provides a similar service. Visit the **companion website (http://www.neal-schuman.com/gis)** for a tutorial on how to use Google Fusion Tables.

Save & Continue, and provide the required information. When completed, you will be forwarded to a page that allows you to download your map as a KML file. This link is available at the very bottom of the page. Click on **Download Digital Air Photo Collection Google Earth (KML)**. Save and then open this file in Google Earth.

Figure 5.8. Table Geocoded in Google Maps

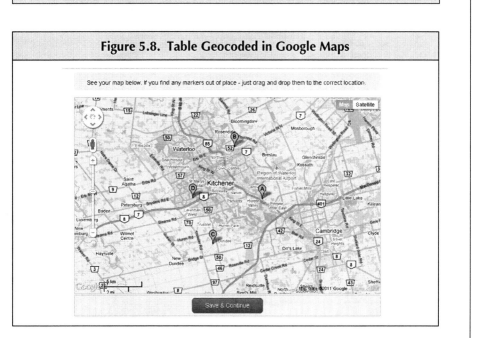

Modifying Contents of Placemarks

When you open the KML file in Google Earth, you will notice that the placemarks are represented by the default yellow pushpins. This can easily be changed. However, first take a look at how your tabular rows and columns are being represented in your placemarks. Click on a placemark. Figure 5.9 shows how the tabular information looks displayed in Google Earth.

147

Figure 5.9. Results of the Geocoded Table Displayed in Google Earth

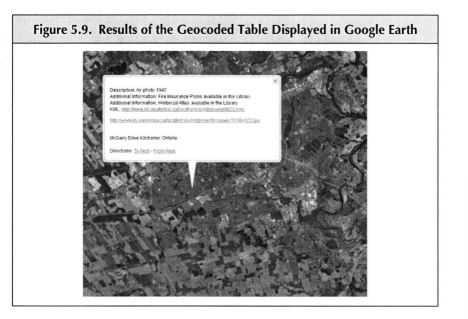

You can modify each placemark icon independently by expanding your folder in the Table of Contents, right clicking on each placemark, and selecting **Properties**. Here you can not only customize your icon, but you can also edit or add additional information to the placemark.

For a customized icon, you may wish to use the image of the document that the placemark is representing. Simply click on **Add Custom Icon** and add the URL of the digitized image. Google Earth will automatically scale the image down to an appropriate icon size. For additional affect, you may wish to add the actual image to the placemark description. To do this, simply add the following code underneath the rest of the information you have transferred over into the description box: <img src="add the link of your image here">.

To embed this map into your library website, you will need to download the Google Earth Plugin and its JavaScript API. This is very easy to do, as it requires only few additional lines of script added to your webpage. Instructions on how to do this are available from http://code.google.com/apis/earth/. Once you have included the API into your HTML code, your library users will be able to use Google Earth directly from your library's webpage.

Alternatively, another way to embed your collection of placemarks into your webpage is to import your KML file into Google Maps' My Maps. Chapter 3 discussed how to embed a map into a website.

Georeferencing Collections

Georeferencing documents requires quite a bit more effort than geocoding, as it is assigning precise geographic coordinates to the digital document. Whereas geocoding is adding a location stamp to an approximate location on the earth, georeferencing is much more accurate, requiring special software and application tools do so. Maps, aerial photography, and satellite imagery are the only types of documents that are georeferenced, because they can be accurately draped over the earth. A specific feature on a map can be matched to the same feature on the Earth, thereby providing an accurate connection between the two.

The combination of aerial photography and georeferencing technology brings traditional air photo interpretation to a higher level. When an image is georeferenced to the earth's surface, the user can overlay additional geospatial datasets. It may be land use information, census data, recent air photo imagery, current streets, property boundaries, and so forth. If a particular feature on a photo is not clear, one can confirm its identification by overlaying relative data such as the street network. With the GIS tools available, a user can compare the past and the present with very close precision. If the user is interested in studying the loss of forestry, for example, one can overlay an historical aerial photograph on top of a more recent one to study the changes and discover precisely where new trees could be planted.

Georeferencing an image requires the user to identify several points on the photo. The user will initially need to locate a point of reference to get geographical bearings. Street intersections make excellent reference points, as they have specific points that need to be connected or "referenced" to the same intersection point on a current

> **Georeferencing-Supported Software Programs**
>
> Any paper aerial photograph, map, or index can be scanned and georeferenced to be used in a GIS program or in online programs such as Google Earth/Maps. Georeferencing is completed in GIS software programs such as Esri's ArcGIS, TatukGIS Editor, and free products like DIVA-GIS, MapWindow GIS, QGIS, and Mapmaker. See the **companion website (http://www .neal-schuman.com/gis)** for more information.

street map. Many users find using streets or rivers helps identify the location of the photos. The GIS program records the coordinates of each point and thereby tags the photo and applies a specific spatial reference system to it.

Although it is important to realize the value of georeferencing, it is not something that most library staff will be in a position to do; therefore, a tutorial on georeferencing is not included in this book. For those interested in georeferencing, a tutorial on georeferencing using ArcGIS and Google Earth is available on the **companion website (http://www.neal-schuman.com/gis)**.

Sharing Geospatial Resources in KML Format

Geospatial resources are a valuable addition to the library collection; however, when the files are stored physically on library servers in their original shapefile format, most library users will never find the opportunity to take advantage of them. Geospatial files need to be freed of their limiting traditional storage devices, and, as many libraries have already done, they need to be made freely accessible online. Geospatial files made available only in their native shapefile format will attract only GIS users, however. Because these files are potentially beneficial to all Internet users, it's more common now to see these files available also in KML format.

There are a number of ways to convert a shapefile to KML format. Some libraries convert them and share them online, and others convert them when the need arises from reference requests. The following tutorials may prove helpful to those wanting to expose their GIS collection or wanting to increase the potential of mapping in Google Earth. For any library user not interested in using shapefiles, the following translation programs will enable them to take advantage of the files in Google Earth.

Two programs will be reviewed in this section. One can be downloaded freely online and is a shapefile to KML stand-alone converter. The second one uses a shapefile to KML conversion utility in the GIS software program ArcGIS.

Shp2kml: Zonum Solutions

Shp2kml (http://www.zonums.com/shp2kml.html), created by Zonum Solutions, is a stand-alone application that converts Esri shapefiles to Google Earth

KML files. It offers the customization of each individual feature, specified by the user—the symbol, color, width, classification field, and labeling preferences. Shp2kml supports shapefiles in latitude/longitude coordinates or in the Universal Transverse Mercator coordinate system and accepts all points, lines, and polygons.

To get a sense of how the Zonum shp2kml application works, you will need to download the application onto your computer (available from http://www.zonums.com/shp2kml.html), as well as download a number of shapefiles from the web. The website Map Cruzin (2011) has a large number of GIS files available for download. You will be working with shapefiles for Alaska. Connect to http://www.mapcruzin.com/free-united-states-shapefiles/free-alaska-arcgis-maps-shapefiles.htm, and download the following shapefiles:

- Alaska Administrative Boundaries
- Alaska Highway
- Alaska Water

Unzip all the files to prepare them for the conversion. Start the shp2kml application on your computer. You will notice that shp2kml comes in two components. On the left side you will have the converter, and on the right side you will have the preview map, showcasing your results (Figure 5.10). To begin the conversion of your shapefiles to KML, click on **Input File** and locate the Alaskan administrative boundaries. Accept the default coordinate system and datum and click on **Next**.

At this stage you can specify the details that you would like to appear in Google Earth. If you would like to have text appear as you hover your mouse over the icon, select **Mouse Roll over Effect**. If you would like to take advantage of the

Figure 5.10. Zonum Solutions' shp2kml Application

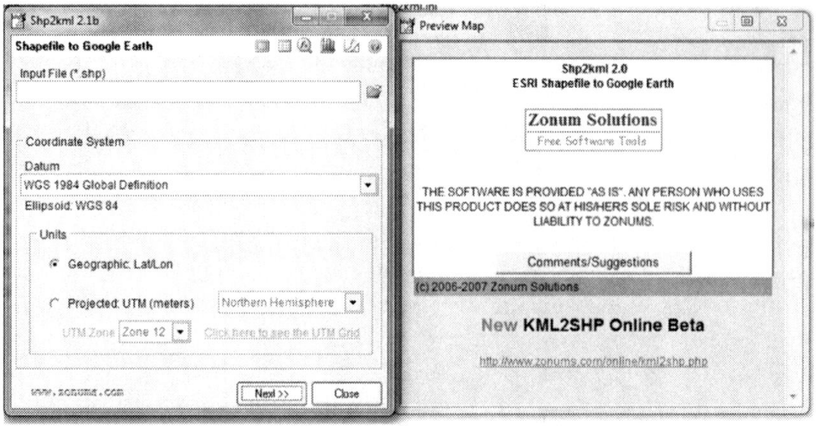

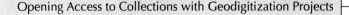

Figure 5.11. Assigning Labels to a KML File in Zonum Solutions' shp2kml Application

Shp2kml 2.1b

Shapefile to Google Earth

Entity Properties

☐ Mouse Roll over Effect

Field Label   NAME ▼

Display Label   ☐ Always   ☐ Roll over   ☑ Never

Polygon Roll over effect

☐ Do not Change Style   ☑ Change Color

☐ Create polygon centroid

☐ A centroid for each Polygon when multigeometry

Symbology

☑ Single Symbol   ☐ Unique Value   ☐ Graduate Value

www.zonums.com   [<< Back]   [Next >>]   [Close]

151

labels available from the attribute table, select the **Field Label** to be **Administrative Level** and make the label active only upon mouse roll over. However you will find that selecting these features will clutter the map with placemarks, so, for this tutorial, keep both features turned off (Figure 5.11).

If the feature had a number of categories available that would be worthwhile to group together and display as individual groups, you may want to select the symbology to be categorized as a **unique value**; however, because this feature is a line file, keep it as **single symbol** and click **Next**. Select a color for the administrative boundaries and change the line width to **3**. Click on **Next**. When users click on the file, a balloon will pop up with attribute information. Select all the tabular columns you would like displayed in the attribute balloon. In this example, select both columns available (Figure 5.12).

Provide a title for your layer, such as **Administrative Boundaries**. Select a color for your pop-up balloon, and activate **Show Table Borders** in order to organize your attribute information. Adjust the colors of the table to your liking, and click on **Next** when finished.

Figure 5.12. Select Variables to Include in the Attribute Balloon in Zonum Solutions' shp2kml Application

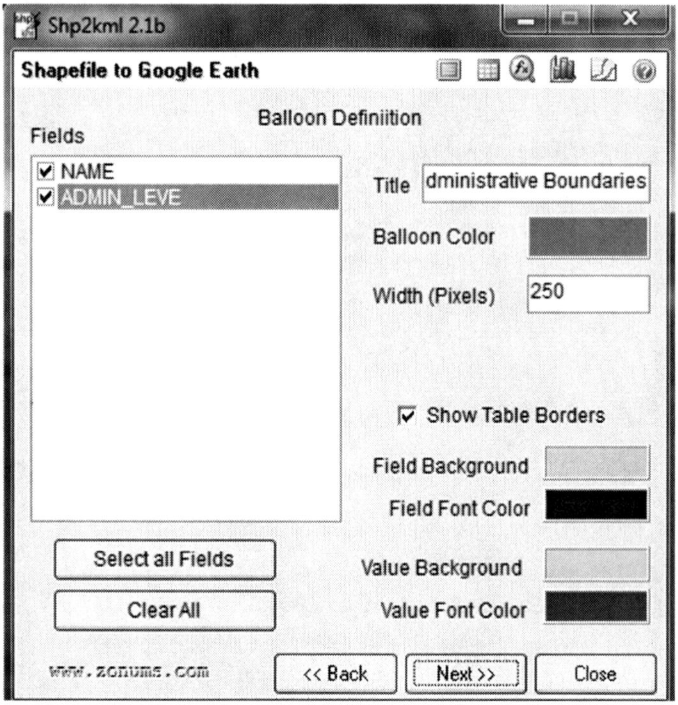

In this section, you are asked to provide a name and description for your layer. For name, type in **Alaskan Administrative Boundaries**, and add a description if you wish. Clicking on **Create KML File** will prompt you to save the file to your local computer. Once you have done that, you can open it in Google Earth to see what your results look like.

Repeat this procedure for the other two shapefiles. Then, gather all three files and open them in Google Earth. Figure 5.13 shows what the shapefiles converted to KML files may look like. Clicking on any of the files will bring up their attribute information (Figure 5.14).

The color and size of the KML features can be customized at this point as well. Right clicking on the KML file from the Table of Contents will provide you with access to the layer properties. From there you can customize the layer's style and color.

After files have been converted to KML format, they can be individually offered for download online. You can offer them either in a tabular format or in a map format with clickable placemarks. Either way, making your geospatial collection accessible to the general public in a popular and easy to use format will certainly increase the number of users exposed to both geographic files and Google Earth.

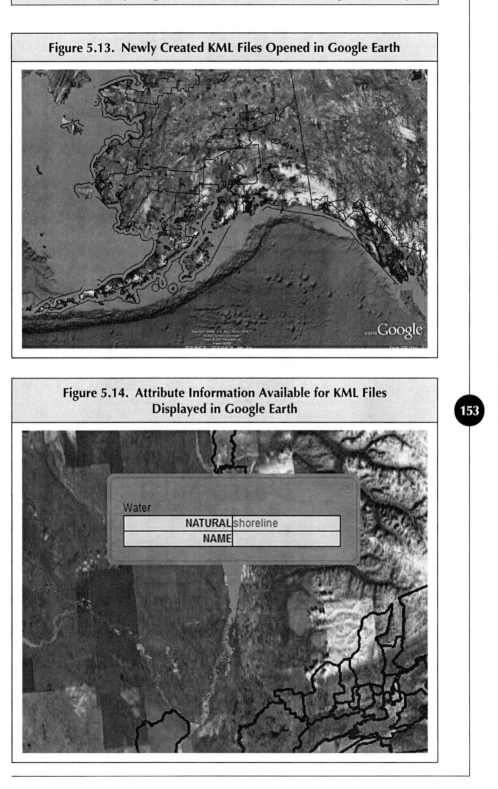

Figure 5.13. Newly Created KML Files Opened in Google Earth

Figure 5.14. Attribute Information Available for KML Files Displayed in Google Earth

153

Water

NATURAL	shoreline
NAME	

Shapefile to KML Converter in ArcGIS

An alternative application to use for converting shapefiles to KML files is Esri's ArcMap, as it has an built-in utility conversion tool. If users have access to ArcMap, then it may be easier for them to use this product over the shp2kml application from Zonum, as it requires fewer steps.

This tutorial will be using the same data files for Alaska that were used in the previous tutorial. To begin, start ArcMap, and begin a new map session. Before you begin the conversion, you will add all the data layers of interest into the program. This will enable you to visualize the layers and get a sense of what the KML files will look like.

To add the three Alaskan shapefiles, click on **File** and then **Add Data**, and navigate to the folder where you have saved your files. When you have successfully added the files, you are ready to begin converting them to KML format.

On the right side of the program, there is a Search button. You will locate the KML conversion tool using the Search button. Click on the button and in the Search field type in **KML** and click on the **magnifying glass** to activate the search (Figure 5.15).

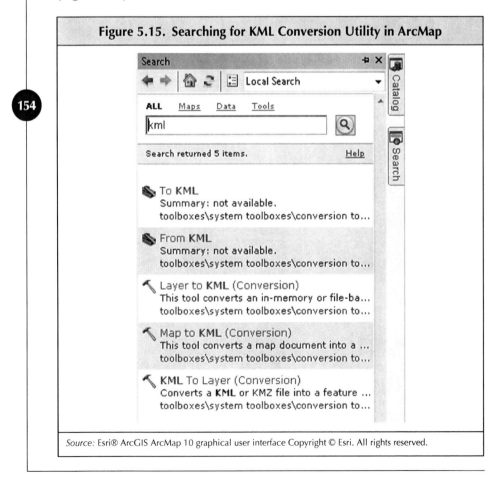

Figure 5.15. Searching for KML Conversion Utility in ArcMap

Source: Esri® ArcGIS ArcMap 10 graphical user interface Copyright © Esri. All rights reserved.

Figure 5.16. KML Conversion Utility in ArcMap 10

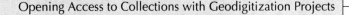

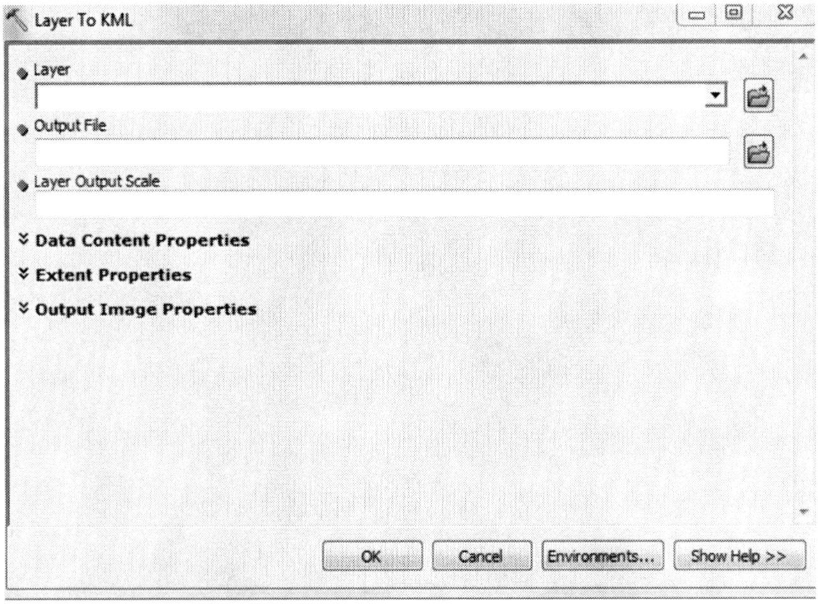

From the list of search results, select **Layer to KML (Conversion)**. This will bring up the conversion utility (Figure 5.16). You can now easily locate the layer that you would like to convert by clicking on the **down arrow icon** to select from the list available in your table of contents. Begin with the administrative boundaries. Your **Output File** will be the location where you would like your new KML file to be saved. Navigate to a folder on your computer and give your new KML file an appropriate file name. The **Layer Output** scale is the scale that you would like to export the layer. Any scale will work; however, 1,000 is typical. Click **OK** to begin the conversion. This may take anywhere from a few seconds to a few minutes.

Repeat this process with the other two shapefiles, and, when completed, open your newly created KML/KMZ files in Google Earth. Figure 5.17 shows what your KML files may look like. If you expand the KML files in the Table of Contents, you will notice that the attribute information has transferred over as well. Clicking on any KML feature on the map will also activate the table, popping up its information in a window.

The color and size of the KML features can be customized at this point as well. Right clicking on the KML file from the Table of Contents will provide you with access to the layer properties. From there you can customize the layer's style and color.

Figure 5.17. Newly Created KML Files Displayed in Google Earth

Other KML Conversion Utilities

The two shapefile to KML conversion applications reviewed are fairly basic, but they do a quick and simple job. Other conversion programs offer more advanced options, primarily glorifying the pop-up balloon styles and providing advanced labels and symbology, legend creations and logos, and 3D support. ArcGIS, version 9.3, offers a sophisticated utility, aside from the basic one described earlier, which needs to be installed into the program as a script. Export to KML 2.5.4 ArcScript can be downloaded from http://arcscripts.esri.com/details. asp?dbid=14273. A guide on how to use this conversion tool is available on the **companion website (http://www.neal-schuman.com/gis)**.

For those without access to ArcGIS, the professional version of Google Earth (Google Earth Pro) does a fabulous job with the conversions as well. Google Earth Pro is a $400 upgraded version of Google Earth, offering users the ability to directly import shapefiles into the

---

Google Earth Pro Features

Google Earth Pro has a number of upgraded features, making it a more sophisticated mapping program than its free version. Besides its ability to import shapefiles, it also imports georeferenced images such as GeoTIFFs and GPS points. Google Earth Pro also allows users to save images in a higher resolution and has better printing options as well.

program. Once the files are displayed in the program, they can easily be converted into KML files. Google Earth Pro is often distributed to educational institutions free of charge, so libraries may wish to contact Google to obtain this program.

A few other shapefile to KML conversion programs are available for free online. For a review of some of these conversion programs, visit http://spatialnews.geocomm.com/articles/overviewofkmlconversionprograms/.

Conclusion

Mapping technology is used in several library websites and digital projects, providing an innovative search and delivery service to library users. Google technology is by far the most popular, offering interfaces that allow for easy project creation and easy use by patrons and clients. Geodigitization projects are expanding the library's user base, offering resources online with familiar Web 2.0 technology. This chapter has highlighted just a few of the many libraries that are using geotagging and mapping technology to link library resources to a relevant location in the community, the city, or the world. This chapter has offered several tutorials to help library staff get started on their own geodigitization projects. The **companion website (http://www.neal-schuman.com/gis)** includes several additional tutorials for some of the more advanced mapping projects.

A few years ago, several map libraries started taking advantage of GIS technology and methodology to showcase and deliver their library locations. Today, non-GIS library staff, non-map libraries, and many public libraries have embraced the technology to promote and deliver their own library's resources. With Google's commitment to broadening the user base of GIS and mapping technology, geodigitization has never been so easy and accessible, increasing the use of and demand for library resources.

157

References

Brenner, Michaela, and Peter Klein. 2008. "Discovering the Library and Google Earth." *Information Technology and Libraries*, June 1, 27: 2.

Jacobsen, Mikael. 2008. "Google Maps: You Are Here." *Library Journal* (October 15). http://www.libraryjournal.com/article/CA6602836.html.

Map Cruzin. 2011. "Free GIS Shapefiles, Software, Resources and Geography Maps." Map Cruzin. Accessed April 4. http://www.mapcruzin.com/.

Markey, Karen. 2007. "The Online Library Catalog: Paradise Lost and Paradise Regained?" *D-Lib Magazine* 13, no. 1/2 (January/February). http://dlib.org/dlib/january07/markey/01markey.html.

University of Connecticut. 2011. "Connecticut GIS Data @ MAGIC." University of Connecticut Library. Accessed March 28. http://magic.lib.uconn.edu/connecticut_data.html.

University of Vermont. 2011. "Long Trail Photographs." University of Vermont Library. Accessed March 28. http://cdi.uvm.edu/collections/browseCollection.xql?pid=longtrail&title=Long%20Trail%20Photographs.

University of Western Ontario. 2010. "Aerial Photography: London 1922 Online." University of Western Ontario Serge A. Sauer Map Library. Last updated November 29. http:// geography.uwo.ca/maplibrary/airphoto/london22/google/google_index_1922.htm.

Vandenberg, Michael. 2008. "Using Google Maps as an Interface for the Library Catalogue." *Library High Tech* 26: 1.

Chapter 6

Expanding and Enhancing Library Services with GIS

Introduction: Embedding GIS into Library Services

When one thinks about a GIS service in a library, often what comes to mind is a specialized department populated with computers and trained staff assisting users with GIS questions. After all, academic libraries have been offering GIS services to library users for at least 25 years. Although a GIS department or unit is fairly popular among academic libraries, GIS technology is now also disbursed among several library types and various departments and used in library planning and public programs. Public libraries in particular have invested in GIS, especially at the administrative level, assisting in the planning of services and facilities based on neighborhood demographics. More and more public libraries are also establishing new library GIS services, catering to the business community and education sector.

Traditional library services are expanding to include GIS resources, and library programs are being enhanced by the inclusion of GIS technology in the planning and delivery of them. From offering Google Earth workshops to geocaching activities to seminars on using maps for genealogical research, libraries are introducing their users to mapping and GIS-based resources. Libraries are a source of information and education, as demonstrated by their offering of training seminars, instruction support, and personal assistance in finding and using map-based resources.

This chapter will examine how academic and public libraries utilize GIS technology and mapping resources in library programs, in teaching, and in learning. This chapter will also offer considerations for establishing a basic GIS information service and training opportunities for library staff.

Incorporating GIS into Library Instruction Programs

Whether public and academic library users realize it or not, GIS and mapping technology has been introduced to many of them in the past recent years.

Through creative library programming, library users have been given the opportunity to gain geospatial information literacy skills.

Many libraries subscribe to and promote map resources; they offer workshops and run activities and events that are developed and delivered using GIS technology. Workshops are one of the more common ways of educating library users on a specific topic. Usually offered free of charge to the library community, workshops vary in theme, style, and duration.

Library Instruction Workshops

Both public and academic libraries often offer workshops for their patrons. Usually library staff plan and deliver the workshops, but occasionally specialists and guests are invited to deliver the workshop. Although workshops are primarily offered to library users to disseminate information and educate users about library resources and related materials, occasionally specialized workshops and presentations are offered to library staff members exclusively for training purposes. Staff training will be discussed later in this chapter.

Perhaps the most popular among both academic and public libraries is an introductory session on the resources and features available in Google Earth and Google Maps. Public libraries such as Cleveland Public Library in Ohio, Woodstock Public Library (2009) in Illinois, Vancouver Public Library (2011), and Haines Borough Public Library (2011) in Alaska encourage users to learn the features available in Google Earth. Some libraries such as Brentwood Public Library in New York offer Google Earth workshops specifically to their genealogical communities, focusing on family history research.

Google Earth and Google Maps tend to be just as, if not more, popular with the academic library users. Mapping workshops and related resources are regularly offered by numerous academic libraries. These are just a few examples:

- University of Texas at Austin (2010) offers a Google Earth workshop focusing on rhetoric and literature (http://www.cwrl.utexas.edu/event/google-earth-workshop).
- Columbia University Libraries (2009) offers a workshop on exporting Google Earth KML/KMZ files and working with these files in ArcGIS (https://blogs.cul.columbia.edu/culspatial/2009/10/30/gis-workshop-working-with-arcgis-google-earth/).
- Massachusetts Institute of Technology (2011) offers a workshop on Google Maps API and KML (http://libraries.mit.edu/gis/teach/previous-workshops.html#google).
- Carleton College (2011) offers resources on teaching geologic map interpretation using Google Earth (http://serc.carleton.edu/NAGTWorkshops/structure/teaching_geo_map_interp.html).

160

- Cornell University (2011) offers an introductory workshop on using Google Earth as well as Google Maps. Topics covered include recording locations of features, changing display styles, and using icons and colors (http://www.library.cornell.edu/svcs/serve/classinst).
- Stony Brook University Library (2008) offers a Google Earth workshop covering mapping, adding external resources, and manipulating KML files (http://library.cc.stonybrook.edu/sbulibraries/?p=219).

Most workshops offer an overview of the features available and highlight the significance and value of the ability to import external KML files into the program for further mapping capabilities. In addition to Google Earth and Google Maps, some libraries are also beginning to offer workshops on Google Fusion Tables, the application that geocodes addresses and converts tables into maps. It is clear that many libraries value the ease of use, access, and feature specifications available in Google mapping products, incorporating them into the library's collection of reputable resources.

Although Google's map products are widely used among libraries and library users, there are certainly other mapping and GIS resources that are valued by libraries. The geospatial librarian at the New York Public Library (2011), for example, offered a workshop entitled "Future Library: Socializing History with Maps." This event introduced participants to social geolocation and mapping using historic materials (http://www.amiando.com/smwnynypl1 .htm). In fact, researchers' interests in geolocation and georeferencing has provided historians and genealogists with a larger resource bank, as more and more historical maps are becoming digitized and georeferenced. Several libraries offer workshops and pathfinders on genealogical resources, with many pointing researchers to maps online. University of Colorado at Boulder Library (2011) has created an excellent web guide providing presentations and handouts on using maps in genealogical research (http://ucblibraries.colorado.edu/map/ links/genealogy.htm).

Perhaps the most popular types of GIS and mapping-related workshops offered by academic librarians are GIS software related. Although many institutions offer a variety of workshops on different software products, ArcGIS is by far most commonly delivered. With 2,500 academic libraries using Esri products, and only 500 public libraries using them (Angela Lee, e-mail, April 26, 2011), it is no surprise that academic librarians are leaders in GIS software training.

ArcGIS workshops vary from institution to institution, with some offering students an introduction to mapping and others focusing on specific features of the program, such as georeferencing, geocoding, and spatial analysis. Some also offer workshops that are theme specific, such as the workshop on Public Health GIS offered by the Chanhassen Public Library in Minnesota (http://gis.co.carver .mn.us/website/Public_Health_Workshop/). Some of the more popular topics covered in GIS workshops across North American academic libraries include the following:

- Creating simple maps in ArcGIS
- Working with census data in ArcGIS
- Georeferencing maps with ArcGIS
- Digital elevation modeling in ArcGIS
- Online mapping
- ArcExplorer Desktop and Online
- Open source GIS

Training sessions or workshops should accompany any GIS service offered in a library to assist users in gaining the skills and independence of working with GIS software and spatial data. Because there are so many workshops publicized freely online, library staff should have no problem finding workshop ideas that would meet the needs of their library users. Librarians are encouraged to partner with GIS librarians or GIS specialists to deliver GIS software workshops.

Not all libraries offer an official GIS service, and for some libraries GIS software and data are not necessary. With so many mapping and GIS resources now available online, desktop GIS may one day become obsolete. Previous chapters have discussed the various online resources available to both public and academic library users. Offering instructional sessions on these resources will help develop geospatial literacy skills in library users as well as shed light on many of the wonderful projects, tools, and programs available.

An alternative way to share information and provide library instruction is through library activities and events. Offering a fun and less formal gathering may attract a larger group of library users with various skill sets and interests.

Library Activities and Events

Most libraries have offered some form of activity or event to attract users into the library. Whether it's for promotional purposes, joint efforts with organizations, or teaching and learning purposes, there is usually some degree of fun associated with the activity or event to encourage participation. Some activities may not be at all related to the library, or the library's collection, as some may be designed to encourage networking between library staff and library patrons—perhaps a meet and greet, or a library celebration of some kind.

Offering fun activities or events that are GIS or mapping related provides an interesting and casual way to introduce participants to the concept of GIS or to geolocations and related resources. One of the more popular activities offered in public libraries is

> **Geocaching**
>
> Often described as a high-tech game of hide and seek, geocaching is an outdoor activity that uses navigational devices (GPS units, cell phones) to find hidden containers. Participants are usually given the geographic coordinates of the hidden objects.

location-based gaming, such as geocaching. Becoming more popular with educators, location-based applications are being used to bring fun to learning.

Some libraries offer geocaching events right in their own library, encouraging participants to explore the library building and its resources. The Shoshone Public Library in Idaho has found great success with this game, drawing new community members into the library (Funabiki, 2009). Some libraries also use the game as a way to introduce newcomers to the neighborhood, helping them explore local landmarks and buildings. Because of the popularity of geocaching, some libraries sign out geocaching kits to patrons. West Virginia in particular encourages geocaching, using it as a tool for educating citizens about West Virginia's rich history. Provided by the Department of Education and Arts, the geocaching kits include a GPS receiver, an instruction book, maps, and guides. The GPS devices have geographic coordinates for local caches already preloaded. Several library branches also include hands-on geocaching instruction sessions (McCoy, 2011).

Geocaching activities and workshops are also offered at academic libraries but usually as part of a larger event. One of the most popular GIS-related events hosted by many academic libraries is GIS Day. GIS Day is an international annual grassroots educational event that promotes geographic awareness and showcases real-life uses of GIS. Thousands of organizations worldwide celebrate GIS Day by hosting workshops, poster sessions, and open houses. GIS Day is celebrated by the K–12 educational system as well as by many postsecondary institutions and public and private organizations. GIS Day falls on the third Wednesday in November.

Most GIS Day celebrations hosted by academic libraries include poster sessions that showcase students' GIS work. Students and faculty are often invited to speak at the events, describing their GIS-related research and project work. Libraries have the opportunity to offer hands-on training sessions or activities such as GIS workshops, geocaching, and library exhibits. GIS Day is an excellent promotional event for the library and its GIS resources, as many curious students drop in to learn about the technology and how it could be used for academic purposes.

What's unique about GIS Day is that it is a collective celebration of GIS technology. Hosting GIS Day for the first time may seem daunting; however, with so many experienced library hosts, help isn't too far away. Many online resources offer suggestions for planning and hosting GIS Day. There are templates available for promotional brochures and posters and suggestions for activities, door prizes, and even cake designs.

Celebrating a GIS service, teaching library patrons about spatial resources, and helping develop geospatial information literacy skills can only be accomplished if the library has a GIS service to offer and has trained staff to offer it. The following section will provide guidance to those libraries that do not

163

currently have an established GIS or mapping service. This service can be as simple as having Google Earth installed on library computers or having pathfinders available for online mapping programs. A more advanced service would be offering GIS software resources, such as ArcGIS Explorer or ArcGIS for desktop, a collection of geospatial data resources, and related assistance with the products.

Implementing GIS Services in the Library

A large number of academic libraries today already have an established GIS service. GIS was first introduced to libraries in 1992, when a coordinated project by the Association of Research Libraries (ARL) and the Environmental Systems Research Institute (Esri) encouraged the use of the large mass of geospatial data that was being made available from the federal government. Before library staff could be trained on using the data, they first needed access to and training on using GIS software. The coordinated project, called the GIS Literacy Project, offered free GIS software from Esri as well as staff training with the aims of educating and equipping librarians with the skills needed to provide library users access to GIS data. With their newly gained skills and software programs, libraries were left to develop a GIS delivery service (ARL, 1999).

Since the inception of the GIS Literacy Project, hundreds of libraries have incorporated GIS into their library services. The levels of GIS services offered do vary quite a bit, however. Even the most basic GIS services require trained and knowledgeable staff. Library users assume that staff adopt the role of mentors and trainers and therefore expect to be educated by those offering GIS services. Therefore, it's important to be able to support any resource or product offered at a library. If a mapping program is installed on a public library computer, staff must have working knowledge of the program.

One of the most basic GIS services that one can offer is simply providing users with guides and pathfinders and hands-on assistance with online resources for data, mapping applications, and instruction. Both academic and public libraries will have the opportunity to work with library users who are interested in online mapping resources. This type of library service would prove most successful if all library staff providing Tier 1 service (i.e., at the information or virtual desk) were trained on these resources. Staff should be able to point users to a number of suitable resources available online. The staff member should also have working knowledge of some of the online applications as well in order to successfully transfer knowledge to the patron. Some suggested online sites include municipal websites for interactive mapping, Google Earth/Google Maps, ArcGIS Explorer Online and Desktop, and several of the other online applications mentioned in previous chapters.

A step above this GIS service model is having staff members trained on at least one open source GIS program and making this program available from at least one dedicated computer in the library. The open source program would be a free application that offers user-friendly map making features. Along with the application, the library would also have a collection of GIS data files that can be used in the program or can be copied and used in other programs outside of the library. How-to guides accompanying the GIS computer station would be helpful to the users, along with a list of online data sources. The staff members need to be trained on the basics of map making, GIS files, and the specific GIS program used. Chapter 4 provided an introduction to some of the fundamental cartographic and GIS skills required for map making in a GIS program. The staff member would need to be prepared to teach library users how to use the program and offer basic map making support. If this level of service is offered, a GIS librarian or GIS specialist should be made available to answer specific geographic, cartographic, or GIS questions the librarian or user may have. Although anybody can be trained in the basics of map making, often troubleshooting requires experience.

The GIS service can also include subscription services to mapping programs such as the census online mapping program SimplyMap. Used by both academic and public libraries, subscription-based online mapping resources may require library staff assistance in getting started with the program. Library users may have many technical and map-based questions about the resource, and library staff must be trained to answer these questions. Training may be available from representatives of the products, from peers or colleagues, and through self-training.

The GIS service model that goes beyond free versions of software and self-training consists of the reference model that hundreds of academic libraries are currently following. Most libraries that offer a GIS service will have at least one computer installed with Esri's ArcGIS. Some libraries even have numerous computers available in a classroom or lab setting, populated with GIS software. Additional GIS-related utilities such as shapefile to KML conversions, geographic coordinate system translators, graphic programs, and tabular applications (Excel or Access) may also prove to be beneficial to the user and should accompany the list of software installed on the computers. Because ArcGIS has the capabilities to offer simple mapping, advanced mapping, spatial analysis, and other advanced functions, a staff member with in-depth GIS training should be made available to assist patrons with their mapping needs.

Libraries that have invested money in proprietary software and trained staff members will tend to also develop and maintain their own collection of data resources. Collection development and maintenance is just one of many responsibilities of the staff member(s) working in the GIS library unit. With such a quickly evolving field, staff need to stay afloat of recent developments, applications, and data sets. Quite often they are also responsible for GIS data promotion and software training, leading the development and maintenance of a geospatial information literacy program.

GIS Staff Training

Aside from offering geospatial data and software accessibility, library staff working in a GIS environment also need to offer training and technical support to assist users with the software. Non-GIS librarians are not expected to have this advanced teaching skill, so assistance from a GIS librarian would prove beneficial. Earlier in this chapter examples were provided of the types of workshops that some libraries offer to library users. A final and perhaps most important component of offering a GIS service in a library is providing training support to library staff. Without knowledgeable staff, most library users would not be able to utilize the GIS services offered. A library professional is often required for assistance in using mapping resources, such as online mapping programs, desktop GIS programs, and acquiring GIS data, whether available online or on a library server.

Depending on the type of service offered, some training programs will include all library staff so that basic mapping questions can be answered at the information desk. Some library school programs are offering GIS training to students, so a handful of new librarians will be skilled already. However, those who have not taken mapping or GIS-related courses still have several opportunities to gain or upgrade their mapping skills.

Although several library associations offer online training for librarians, only one has recently offered GIS training. The American Library Association's Reference and User Services Association (RUSA) offers a three-week online course on Spatial Literacy. This course caters to librarians in non-GIS or mapping roles, specifically those who have information desk responsibilities. The course introduces library staff to online mapping resources such as Google Earth, municipal mapping, and map mashups. Library staff are also introduced to the concept of GIS. This is the first course of its kind to offer GIS skills to librarians pursuing postacademic studies.

As was mentioned in Chapter 1, not too many Master of Library Science programs offer GIS courses; however, the numbers are steadily increasing each year. Some of the institutions that have offered courses in GIS include the University of Western Ontario, University of Tennessee, State Ohio University, and the University of Wisconsin–Madison. The courses introduce students to many of the concepts covered in this book: geographic awareness, online mapping, GIS software and data, map making, GIS workshops, and more.

Training opportunities are also available from a number of other avenues and sources. Sometimes in-house training is an option for libraries that are interested in expanding the roles of reference library staff. In-house training can entail offering workshops to reference staff and teaching them the basics of geographic awareness, spatial literacy, online mapping, and GIS. The University of Waterloo is one example of an academic library that has offered GIS information sessions and workshops to its librarians and library associates. Introducing staff to GIS resources will not only broaden their own knowledge of information resources but will also allow them to answer basic GIS questions that used to be answerable only by GIS and map librarians.

In the past several years, themes and topics related to GIS in libraries have been shared with attendees of several North American library conferences. Through poster and paper sessions, GIS library staff members have been educating others on geographic and GIS awareness. Commonly presented are case studies on how GIS is utilized in libraries, in outreach, in digital library projects, and in general reference, providing learning opportunities to both public and academic library staff.

Similarly, many articles have been written about this topic, often published in technological library journals as well as map and GIS publications, such as the *Association of Canadian and Map Library Archives (ACMLA) Bulletin*. Dedicated map and GIS journals often include summaries of the latest GIS trends as well as step-by-step user guides for and reviews of GIS-based software programs.

Networking with other librarians, attending conferences, and signing up for library training sessions are excellent ways to gain cutting edge GIS skills as well as ideas for implementing GIS into the library. For those interested in starting up a formal GIS library service utilizing Esri's GIS software program, one of the most recommended GIS training programs is available through Esri's Virtual Campus (http://training.esri.com/gateway/index.cfm).

Esri offers a number of free and fee-based online training sessions that are GIS software based. A novice user can take one or more online courses and develop many of the technical skills needed to offer a GIS service at a library.

To offer a successful GIS service, library staff need a variety of skills, ranging from the ability to engage in critical thinking to knowledge of different learning styles and teaching methods. Although basic software and data skills are required, it is also highly recommended that library staff stay on top of current geographic awareness and GIS trends. There are many avenues of doing this. Newsgroups and subscriptions to e-mail aliases are an excellent way to stay current and develop networks. Weekly readings of GIS-based blogs or newsletters will provide the librarian with information on GIS-related news, along with service pack releases, new software program news, new data, and new tools and features. The librarian needs to consume this information, digest it, and share it with others as well.

Conclusion

GIS and mapping technology is prevalent is many public and academic libraries. From simple workshops on Google Earth to geocaching events to educational instructional workshops on using GIS software, many libraries are educating the public and academics on current Web Mapping 2.0 technologies. Many libraries are supporting geospatial information literacy and are establishing related programs for both library users and library staff members.

167

Geospatial information literate individuals possess a wide variety of mapping skills that directly relate to their ability to achieve their information-attaining goals throughout their entire lives. They understand and can demonstrate the concepts, principles, and techniques that facilitate geospatial information access and can retrieve, evaluate, and synthesize the information from several sources. The goal is for library staff members to transfer their geospatial information literacy skills to others, as well as complement the library's program with cutting edge GIS-related workshops, activities, events, and supporting pathfinders, guides, and web resources.

This chapter reviewed several public and academic library programs that have incorporated the usage of GIS technology into their programming and activities. Many libraries offer GIS services to their library users through either a formal GIS services department or an informal one that embeds the services within the responsibilities of those staff offering first tier reference services.

This book has introduced library staff to all levels of mapping—from introductions to location-based technologies, to Web 2.0 mapping applications online, to GIS data and mapping in GIS software programs. The information and resources provided will guide libraries and librarians through the steps of training, while providing ideas for enhancing their own library services. Whether it be answering GIS-related questions at the information desk, embedded classroom instruction, promotion and outreach, creating mashups for library websites, delivery of digital library collections, offering workshops and events, or expanding current library services, library staff will have the knowledge and skill sets necessary to comfortably meet the needs of their users. Ongoing training will ensure that library staff are a step ahead of the curve and that they are well versed in modern technology. Location-based technology is only going to become more prominent in society, and libraries are the ideal models for supporting the growth and its use by library users.

References

ARL (Association of Research Libraries). 1999. *The ARL Geographic Information Systems Literacy Project: A SPEC Kit.* SPEC Kit, 238. Washington, D.C.: Association of Research Libraries, Office of Leadership and Management Services.

Carleton College. 2011. "Teaching Geologic Map Interpretation Using Google Earth." Science Education Resource Center. Accessed May 7. http://serc.carleton.edu/ NAGTWorkshops/structure/teaching_geo_map_interp.html.

Columbia University Libraries. 2009. "GIS Workshop—Working with ArcGIS and Google Earth." *CUL Spatial* (blog). October 30. https://blogs.cul.columbia.edu/ culspatial/2009/10/30/gis-workshop-working-with-arcgis-google-earth/.

Cornell University. 2011. "Workshops and Instruction." Cornell University Library. Accessed May 7. http://www.library.cornell.edu/svcs/serve/classinst.

Funabiki. Ruth. 2009. "Geocaching: Hide and Seek at Your Library." *The Idaho Librarian: A Publication of the Idaho Library Association* 59, no. 2. http://www.idaholibraries .org/idlibrarian/index.php/idaho-librarian/article/view/25/81.

Haines Borough Public Library. 2011. "Google Earth." Haines Borough Public Library. Accessed May 7. http://haineslibrary.org/node/121.

Massachusetts Institute of Technology. 2011. "GIS Workshops Previously Offered through MIT GIS Services." Massachusetts Institute of Technology Library. Accessed May 7. http://libraries.mit.edu/gis/teach/previous-workshops .html#google.

McCoy, John. 2011. "Libraries Lend Geocaching Kits to W.Va. Explorers." *The Journal*. April 24. http://www.journal-news.net/page/content.detail/id/560027/Libraries-lend-geocaching-kits-to-W-Va--explorers.html?nav=5004.

New York Public Library. 2011. "Miscellaneous Events: Future Library: Socializing History with Maps." New York Public Library. Accessed May 7. http://www.nypl.org/ audiovideo/future-library-socializing-history-maps.

Stony Brook University Library. 2008. "Google Earth Workshop." *University Libraries News* (blog). September 10. http://library.cc.stonybrook.edu/sbulibraries/?p=219.

University of Colorado at Boulder Library. 2011. "Map Library." University of Colorado at Boulder. Accessed May 7. http://ucblibraries.colorado.edu/map/links/genealogy .htm.

University of Texas at Austin. 2010. "Google Earth Workshop." Digital Writing and Research Lab. http://www.cwrl.utexas.edu/event/google-earth-workshop.

Vancouver Public Library. 2011. "Wired for Learning Workshops: Travel the World with Google Earth." Vancouver Public Library. Accessed May 7. http://www.vpl.ca/ news/details/workshop_wired_for_learning_travel_the_world_with_google_earth.

Woodstock Public Library. 2009. "Google Earth and Conservation." Woodstock Public Library. Last updated August 24. http://www.woodstockpubliclibrary.org/calendar/ google-earth-conservation.

Glossary

ArcGIS: ArcGIS is a Windows-based desktop suite consisting of a group of GIS software products produced by Esri. ArcMap is the most popular application within the suite, used for visualizing, managing, creating and analyzing geographic data.

ArcGIS Explorer Desktop: ArcGIS Explorer Desktop is a free GIS viewer produced by Esri that offers an easy way to explore, visualize, and share GIS information. Local GIS data such as in shapefile format can be added into the program; however, the program also supports the use of data available online. ArcGIS Explorer can be downloaded from http://www.esri.com/software/arcgis/explorer/download.html.

attribute table: An attribute table in a GIS is a tabular file containing rows and columns of information. The table is associated with a class of geographic features so that the locations of each row can be mapped in the GIS program.

basic interactive maps: Basic interactive maps are fairly simplistic maps that have been created by Internet users who have utilized online map making applications. Basic interactive maps are created with very limited functionality, as the program used to create the map will have very few features available besides zooming and other navigational tools.

buffer (GIS): A buffer in GIS is a user-defined area around a map feature, often measured in units of distance. A buffer is often used for proximity analysis.

cartographic elements: Effective visual communication requires the presence of several cartographic elements. These include the map, map title, data citation, north arrow, legend, and scale.

editable interactive maps: An editable interactive map can be created online using an interactive mapping program that supports user imports, edits, and customizability.

Esri: Esri is a software development and services company providing GIS software and geodatabase management applications.

geocaching: Geocaching is an outdoor activity where the participants use a Global Positioning System (GPS) receiver to hide and seek containers (called geocaches).

geocoding: Geocoding is the process of assigning geographic coordinates (in longitude and latitude) to digitized objects using other geographic data, such as street addresses.

geographic coordinate system: A geographic coordinate system is one of the most common coordinate systems used. It is a reference system that uses a three-dimensional spherical surface to determine locations of the earth in degrees of latitude and longitude.

Geographic Information System (GIS): GIS is a set of tools that captures, stores, analyzes, manages, and presents data that are linked to location.

georeferencing: Georeferencing is a procedure used to establish the spatial location of an object (image, map, document, etc.) by linking its position to the earth's surface.

geosocial networking: Geosocial networking is location-based social networking that uses geographic services such as geocoding and geotagging to bring a locational component to social dynamics. User-submitted locations allow social networks to connect with users either in that location or who have similar locational interests.

geospatial analysis: Geospatial analysis is an approach to applying statistical analysis and other informational techniques to geographically based data.

Geospatial Portal (GIS Portal): A Geospatial Portal is a web-based application that offers delivery of spatial data and supporting metadata.

geotagging: Geotagging is the process of adding geographical identification (latitude and longitude coordinates) to objects such as photographs, videos, websites, RSS feeds, and so forth.

GeoWeb: The GeoWeb, or Geospatial Web, is an online environment that supports searching for information based on location instead of subject or keyword.

GIS data (geospatial data): GIS data is a set of files that represent features of the Earth that display in a map format using a GIS software program. GIS data consists of two major parts, spatial and tabular. The spatial component stores information about the type and location of the feature, and the tabular component stores attribute information about the feature.

Global Positioning System (GPS): GPS is an accurate worldwide navigational and surveying facility based on the reception of signals from an array of orbiting satellites.

Google Earth: Google Earth is a free virtual globe, map, and geographic information program that offers a large number of geographic content. Users can virtually visit the entire world using satellite imagery and aerial photography. Users can add their own content such as placemarks, paths, images, text, and KML/KMZ files. Google Earth can be downloaded from http://www.google.com/earth/download/ge/agree.html.

Google Maps: Google Maps is a free web mapping service application and technology provided by Google. Google Maps offers street maps, aerial photography, satellite imagery, and route planning. It also offers information on places and business locations. Google Maps is available from http://maps.google.com/.

Keyhole Markup Language (KML): KML is a geographic file format that displays data primarily in Google Earth and Google Maps, although it is increasingly becoming supported by other mapping applications as well.

map overlay: Map overlay is the process of combining data from two or more maps to generate a new map.

map projection: Map projection is a method of representing the features of the earth on a map. All map projections distort the surface in some fashion, and, depending on the purpose of the map, some are more acceptable than others.

map widget: A widget is a small application that can be installed and executed within a webpage by the end user. When a map widget is installed, the map is displayed on the user's website. Several online map making applications offer map widgets.

mashup: A mashup is an application or webpage that combines content from multiple webpages.

open data: Open data is a philosophy and practice requiring that certain data are freely available to everyone, without restrictions from copyright or other licensing

173

stipulations. Open data relies on liberal licensing that encourages reuse, data discoverability, and data accessibility.

open source GIS: Open source programs are applications that one can access the source code of and build on the original product. Open source GIS programs are an excellent alternative to proprietary GIS products, as they offer many mapping features and are free.

OpenStreetMap: OpenStreetMap is a collaborative project to create a free editable map of the world. The map sections are created using aerial photography, topographic maps, GPS devices, and personal local knowledge. OpenStreetMap is available from http://www.openstreetmap.org/, as well as through a number of online mapping applications.

orthoimage: An orthoimage is a digital georeferenced image of the Earth's surface, taken either from satellite or airborne sensors. Orthoimagery is also commonly referred to as satellite imagery or aerial photography.

personalized interactive maps: A personalized interactive map can be created online using an interactive mapping program that offers a list of selectable features. Personalized interactive maps are created with limited functionality, as the program used to create the map will often have a limited selection of features to select, without support for additional user inputs.

174

Quantum GIS (QGIS): Quantum GIS is a free desktop GIS software application that provides data viewing, editing, map making, and analysis capabilities. It is available for Windows, Mac, Linux, and Unix platforms. QGIS is continually maintained by an active group of volunteer developers who regularly release updates and bug fixes.

raster geospatial files: Raster geospatial files are images, such as jpegs and tiffs, that have been georeferenced to display properly in a GIS program.

Scribble Maps: Scribble Maps is a free online application for users who wish to easily create customized Google Maps. Users can add text, images, points, lines, polygons, placemarks, and more. Final maps can be shared online, as well as embedded into webpages. A more advanced version, Scribble Maps Pro, is also available with registration. Scribble Maps can be used at http://www.scribblemaps.com/.

shapefile: The shapefile is a popular geospatial vector data format for GIS software developed and regulated by Esri.

spatial literacy: Spatial literacy is the ability to use the properties of space to communicate, reason, and solve problems.

static digital maps: Static digital maps are maps available in electronic format that are static and noninteractive.

vector geospatial files: Geospatial data in vector format describes features of the earth as points, lines, and polygons.

volunteered geographic information: *Volunteered geographic information, citizen mapping, volunteer cartography,* and *map crowdsourcing* are popular terms used to describe amateur mapmakers who contribute their knowledge of place and space in GeoWeb applications to build highly detailed maps.

Web Map Service (WMS): A WMS serves georeferenced map images over the Internet that are generated by a map server using data from a GIS database.

web mapping: Web mapping is the process of designing, implementing, generating, and delivering maps on the web.

Index

Page numbers followed by the letter "f" indicate figures.

About the Author

Eva Dodsworth is the Geospatial Data Services Librarian at the University of Waterloo Library where she is responsible for the provision of leadership and expertise in developing, delivering, and assessing geospatial data services and programs offered to members of the University of Waterloo community. Eva's particular interests focus on the promotion, teaching, and training of GIS-related resources to the novice student, faculty, and librarian. Eva is also a part-time instructor at a number of Library and Information Studies Programs in North America. Eva has received her Master of Library and Information Science from the University of Western Ontario.

CPSIA information can be obtained at www.ICGtesting.com
Printed in the USA
BVOW022319151211

278493BV00006B/1/P

839163